TEACHING YOUR CHILD TO TALK TO GOD

Roberta Hromas and Todd Temple

Inspirational Press   New York

Published in 1994 by

Inspirational Press
A division of Budget Book Service, Inc.
386 Park Avenue South
New York, NY 10016

Inspirational Press is a registered trademark of Budget Book Service, Inc.

Published by arrangement with Thomas Nelson Inc., Publishers.

Library of Congress Catalog Card Number: 93-80396

ISBN: 0-88486-096-5

Printed in the United States of America.

Contents

I. Teaching Your Child to Pray

My cherished grandchildren who have heard the comforting words of prayer daily since before they were born. In the order they were sent from heaven:

Christina Danielle
Christopher Alan
Jonathan Michael
Joshua Robert
Rachel Elizabeth

Christina, seven years old, and Jonathan, four, sat down with me one afternoon as I was outlining this book and gave me two pages of suggestions about what I should write for you. We believe our grandchildren were chosen by God and sent to our family to nurture and train in His ways. What a privilege to love them and pray with them!

My heart is especially grateful to my mother, Pauline Parham, who taught me how to pray, so that I could in turn teach our children, Robert Alan and Lee Ann, who have loved and followed the Lord, and now they are teaching my grandchildren.

● Contents

● Introduction

Teaching your child to pray is one of the most important things that you will ever do. Make it a priority in your life!

What is prayer? Prayer is the way God has chosen to communicate with us and to bless us as His children by answering our requests. Prayer spans the world and unites earth with heaven.

Prayer is talking freely to God out of the depths of your heart. It is truly heartfelt, soul-to-soul communication with our heavenly Father. It is communication that deepens, intensifies, and enlarges our foundational relationship with God as our Father. Prayer with other believers has the same benefit; we grow in our spiritual relationship with those who also love Him. No other form of communication will give your child more joy or fulfillment in life.

- Prayer is expressing to God your fears, worries, and concerns.
- Prayer is discussing with Him your problems, needs, and questions.
- Prayer is sharing with Him your joys and delights.

In teaching your child how to pray, assure your child that the Lord is *always* listening for your child's prayers. He is always available. Not only does He hear your child pray, He understands the motives and feelings of your child's heart. Not only does He understand, He responds—and always for your child's good.

Prayer is the most intimate form of communication that your child will ever experience. It is the one thing that your child can do that continually opens your child up to experiencing more and more of God's presence, His healing power, His joy, His unlimited love, and His impenetrable security.

Why does your child *need* to know how to pray?

- Prayer is the key to wholeness and to a feeling of total well-being.
- Prayer is the one thing your child can do that will have great impact on the extending of God's kingdom on this earth, no matter what other skills and talents he may have.
- Prayer is the one thing that your child will be doing on this earth that he will also be doing in heaven.

Make prayer spontaneous, free-flowing, and the natural, first response of your child to any experiences he has in life. In so doing, your child will develop the ability to "pray without ceasing" (1 Thess. 5:17). In so doing, prayer will become a firm foundation for everything else that your child ever does, says, or becomes.

And thus, prayer becomes the center of your child's entire life, the core of her spiritual being.

How can you best teach your child to pray? By praying! This book presents over fifty simple ways. Use them as a beginning point. The more your child prays, the easier it will be for her to pray and the more she will learn about prayer.

In teaching your child to pray, you must recognize that *knowing* about prayer, *thinking* about prayer, and even *thinking up* prayers are not the same as actually praying. There is no substitute for the *doing* of what this book calls upon you to do.

Finally, we need to recognize at the outset of this book that, ultimately, your child will learn most of what he knows about praying by watching and listening to *you* pray. So, let your child overhear you talking to God. Be free to pray with, for, and in the presence of your child. Invite your child to join you in prayer. Pray together as a family.

And again, I encourage you . . . pray! You will never regret the hours of your life that you spend in this glorious pursuit.

1 ● Pray for Forgiveness

Have mercy upon me, O God,
According to Your lovingkindness;
According to the multitude of Your tender mercies,
Blot out my transgressions.
Wash me thoroughly from my iniquity,
And cleanse me from my sin.
        —Psalm 51:1–2

Perhaps no more important prayer will ever be prayed by your child than the one he prays after realizing that he has sinned and, thus, needs to be forgiven by the Lord.

Parents often ask, "When should a child pray a 'sinner's' prayer?"

- When he feels a need to have his *own* relationship with the Lord.
- When he questions whether he will go to heaven.
- When he feels guilty about doing something that he knows is wrong.
- When the child is sorry for doing something and is afraid that he will do it again or won't be able to stop doing it.
- When a child expresses a concern about whether he has a relationship with the Lord.

That's the time to lead your child in this prayer or one similar to it:

Dear Heavenly Father, thank You for sending Jesus to die to take away my sins. I want to accept that gift of love that You have given to me. Send the Holy Spirit to live in my heart and take away from me all the things that I do that displease You. Please forgive me of all my sins. I want to be Your child forever.

Help me to learn more about You and to want to talk to you in prayer every day. Please give me a desire to read the Bible. I pray this in the name of Jesus. Amen.

Assure your child that this is one prayer that the Lord *always* hears and answers with a "Yes, I forgive you."

2 • Praise God for Who He Is

Holy, holy, holy,
Lord God Almighty,
Who was and is and is to come!
—Revelation 4:8

The Lord takes delight in the praises of your child. It is your child's high privilege to praise the Lord for who He is, and to declare the excellence of His name! Teach your child about the nature of God by praising and worshiping God for the attributes He displays. Praise Him for:

• His almighty power.

Children understand the concept of "all mighty." God is mightier than all the armies of all the nations on earth. He is mightier than all the kings and presidents and prime ministers. He is mightier than all the ministers of all the churches around the world. He is mightier than any weapon ever created, any storm that rages in the night, any volcano or earthquake or roaring forest fire. God has all power, all might!

> *We praise you, O God, for your wonder-working power that is mightier than anything that the enemy of our souls might attempt to throw at us to destroy us, kill us, or steal from us!*

- His all-seeing eye.

Teach your child that God sees him at all times, day or night. God knows the innermost thoughts and feelings of your child. It is not possible to keep a secret from Him. His face is always toward us.

> *We praise you, O God, for your tender, watchful care over us and for seeing every detail, circumstance, problem, and joy of our lives!*

- His unlimited love.

Assure your child that God loves him. Nothing that your child does or says can diminish the love that God has for him.

> *We praise you, O God, for your lovingkindness that is always extended to us. Thank You for loving us, for creating us, for giving us life, for sending us Your Son to show us just how much you care about every part of our lives.*

- His eternal and available presence.

Assure your child that he can live with God in heaven forever and ever and ever and ever. Assure your child that God is available to him at any second of any minute of any hour of any day. God is in the moment; He is everlasting.

We praise you, O God, for Your presence with us today . . . and every day of eternity.

Encourage your child to learn more and more about God so he can praise God for more and more of His attributes. Make this your child's prayer:

Help me to know more about You every day of my life.

The more a child learns about the nature of God—through reading the Scriptures, prayer, and fellowship with other believers—the more your child will know all that God wants to be *to* your child and all that He wants to do *for* your child.

3 • Pray to the Heavenly Father

Our Father in heaven . . .
—Matthew 6:9

Encourage your child to address God as his "heavenly Father." Why? The number-one reason is that this is how Jesus taught us to pray and this is how Jesus referred to God. Time and again in the Scriptures we read where Jesus called God "heavenly Father" (Matt. 6:14, 26, 32; 15:13, 16:17, 18:35, among many others).

Second, children can relate to God as a heavenly Father, even if they have not had a good earthly father as a role model of fatherhood. They understand what a father is *supposed* to be and what a heavenly Father *can* be to them.

- "Abba," which means "Father" or "Daddy" in the original language of the New Testament, is One who *provides for and protects His eternal family.*

Share with your child the stories from the Bible that tell of God's provision, many of which can be found in the Exodus story: manna in the wilderness for the children of Israel, a pillar of fire for light by night and cloud of protection from the sun by day to guide them as they traveled to the Promised Land, victories over enemies that tried to destroy them. Assure your child that what

God provided for those "children," He'll also provide for them!

> *Thank you, heavenly Father, for giving me the things that I need. Thank you for keeping me safe and warm and protected.*

• *Abba (Father) is available day and night, forever and ever.*

Every child I've ever met wishes he could spend more time with his father. The heavenly Father is always available. He can always be reached.

> *Thank You, heavenly Father, that I can talk to You any time of the night or day, and anywhere I happen to be.*

• *Abba is infinitely capable.*

God, our Father in heaven, can be and do infinitely more than any earthly father can be or do. He is the perfect Father. He is the ultimate Caregiver. His love is unlimited. His patience is unending. His understanding and compassion are beyond measure. His abilities are unmatched.

> *Thank you, heavenly Father, for doing for me all those things that I can't do for myself or by myself. Thank you for sending Jesus to show me how You*

*want me to live my life. Thank you for loving me
even when I fall short of His example.*

As your child prays to his heavenly Father, he will
develop a concept of a spiritual family. As God becomes
more and more "Father" to your child, other believers
in Him will seem more and more like brothers and sisters. Give your child the wonderful gift of an extended
family that shares common goals and desires, a common outlook on the world, and a similar code of ethics.

4 • Pray in the Name of Jesus

God also has highly exalted Him and given Him the name which is above every name, that at the name of Jesus every knee should bow.

—Philippians 2:9–10

Jesus. All authority in heaven and earth has been given in His name. And we, as disciples, friends, and His redeemed younger brothers and sisters, have been given the privilege of using His name.

• The name of Jesus is to be used only for good.

His name is only to be linked with that which is beneficial, healing, or a blessing to others.

> *Heavenly Father, I ask You in the name of Jesus to heal my friend of this flu. Take away the fever that is making her so hot and uncomfortable. Heal her upset stomach in the name of Jesus.*

• The name of Jesus is only to be used in a prayerful, respectful way.

It must never be used in vain or spoken flippantly. Using the name of Jesus is serious business. You are asking heaven to take action.

Heavenly Father, I ask You in the name of Jesus to protect us as we take this hike in the woods. Send your angels to surround us and watch over us. Keep us from all harm.

I recently heard the story of a girl in China who was caught in a rock slide. Her body was so battered and crushed that her doctor covered her face with a sheet and had given up on her until he heard her whispering, "Jesus, Jesus." At that, he asked the nurse to clean her wounds. Much to his surprise, he entered her hospital room the next morning and saw her sitting up in bed, eating breakfast. He exclaimed, "The organs of your body were so mangled, how is it that you can sit up in bed and eat?" She said softly and reverently, "Just my Jesus."

The physician himself is the one who told me this story, and he concluded it by telling me that he had come to know Jesus as his personal Savior through this experience.

- The name of Jesus is to be used against the enemy —the devil, the father of lies—and not against people.

Discuss the difference with your child. We are to love people but not their sin. We are to value people but take a stand against the evil that may be manipulating their lives or blinding their eyes.

Heavenly Father, I pray in the name of Jesus that You would destroy the evil that is causing this person to be mean to me. Free them from the power of the devil.

As Jesus Himself said, "Whatever you ask in My name, that I will do, that the Father may be glorified in the Son." (John 14:13).

5 ● Pray at Bedtime

And these words which I command you today shall be in your heart; you shall teach them diligently to your children, and shall talk of them when you sit in your house . . . when you lie down.

—Deuteronomy 6:6-7

Perhaps the most famous children's prayer of all time is "Now I lay me down to sleep, I pray the Lord my soul to keep. Should I die before I wake, I pray the Lord my soul to take." Unfortunately, this prayer is *not* one that brings comfort to many of the children who know it and say it. Bedtime is when a child's attention should be diverted to life, not death, to assurance, not fear, to goodness, not worry.

This is often the time of day when children are most likely to express to you their innermost feelings, thoughts, hurts, and concerns. They are eager to put down their own worries and fears.

Children often carry burdens they don't need to carry. They frequently hear just enough about an issue or a family difficulty to begin to worry about it. Encourage your child to use prayer as a forum for airing these concerns directly to God or to you in the form of prayer requests.

Beyond addressing your child's personal questions, problems, and fears, make bedtime prayers an opportunity for your child to:

• Give thanks for the good things of the day.

Thank you that I got to go to the park this afternoon to play with my friends.

• Remember family members in prayer.

Thank you for Mommy, Daddy, Ralphie, and Jenny. Thank you that Daddy got to come home early tonight. Please heal Mommy's cold.

• Ask for protection through the night.

Keep us safe in our house tonight. Help us to have a good night's sleep.

Include a prayer against bad dreams. Encourage your child to ask the Lord to guard his mind during the night hours.

Keep me from having any nightmares; let me dream only good dreams.

• Pray about the challenges of the next day.

Help me remember the right answers as I take my test tomorrow.

Tuck your child into bed with a hug, a kiss, and a prayer. Make it a habit. Your child will thank you for doing so all his life.

6 ● Pray When You Rise Up

These words which I command you today shall be in your heart; you shall teach them diligently to your children . . . when you rise up.

—Deuteronomy 6:6–7

Teach your child to begin her day in prayer. Even before your child gets out of bed, she can say,

Good morning, Jesus. Thank you for today!

Set aside a time during the morning rush to come together as a family for prayer. It may be as you are finishing breakfast or just before the children head off for school or even as you are driving on the way to school. This is a good time to pray the Lord's Prayer together as a family.

Our Father in heaven,
Hallowed be Your name.
Your kingdom come.
Your will be done
On earth as it is in heaven.
Give us this day our daily bread.
And forgive us our debts,
As we forgive our debtors.
And do not lead us into temptation,

> *But deliver us from the evil one.*
> *For Yours is the kingdom and the*
> *   power and the glory forever.*
> *Amen.*

—Matthew 6:9–13

Every child could know the Lord's Prayer by the time she enters first grade. There really is no more complete prayer we can voice to God.

In establishing morning as a prayer time, you may want to teach your child to "put on the whole armor of God," as presented in Ephesians 6:6–12. You can encourage your child to do this as she is dressing for the day. One way to instill the meaning of this concept into your child is to teach your child to say each piece of the armor as described in the Scripture passage and add a one-sentence prayer as she puts on a similar item of her own clothing. For example, as your son puts on his pants or your daughter a skirt,

> *I'm covered with truth. Help me, heavenly Father, to learn only Your truth today.*

Encourage your child also to pray about any specific needs or challenges that he is facing during the coming day.

> *Lord, help me to do my best in school. Keep me in health and bring me home safely at the close of the day.*

The problems may be ongoing ones. Encourage your child to pray about a problem each morning until it is no longer a problem. Recently a friend of mine had dinner with her five-year-old goddaughter, Laurie, who confided, "Nobody likes me at my new school." Laurie was feeling extremely alienated and lonely. My friend encouraged her to pray every morning as she got ready for school.

> *Heavenly Father, help the other children to be nice to me and to include me in their playtime. Help me to make friends.*

Within a week, Laurie reported back that two girls had asked her to play with them every day that week. She was glowing with confidence.

Many parents are concerned only that their children leave for school with sufficiently warm clothing and lunch money in their pockets. Be equally concerned that your children face their days with a covering of prayer and the peace of the Lord in their hearts.

7 ● Pray at Mealtimes

Jesus took the five loaves and the two fish, and looking up to heaven, He blessed and broke and gave the loaves to the disciples; and the disciples gave to the multitudes.

—Matthew 14:19

Jesus recognized that all food comes from the Father and is worthy to be "hallowed" or consecrated by God for use in our bodies. Food sustains life; life is a gift from God; and our lives are precious to God. That's what a mealtime blessing is all about.

Use mealtime prayers as a way of teaching your children to recognize that God is the creator of life, the sustainer of life, and the provider of all that we need in life. One of the most ancient mealtime blessings is the gracious one from Psalm 104. It is often said by Jewish people today:

Blessed art thou, Lord our God, King of the Universe, Who bringeth forth bread out of the earth.

You may want to teach your children a mealtime blessing that they can sing. Some families sing the doxology:

Praise God from whom all blessings flow. Praise Him all creatures here below. Praise Him above ye heavenly hosts. Praise Father, Son, and Holy Ghost.

Another beautiful mealtime prayer song is this one taken from Psalm 145. It is often said responsively.

> *The eyes of all wait upon thee, O Lord,*
> *And thou givest them their meat in due season.*
> *Thou openest Thine hand*
> *And fillest all things living with plenteousness.*

Mealtime prayers provide three wonderful learning opportunities for your child:

- *Practice in praying publicly.*

The more your child prays aloud in the presence of others, the more comfortable he will become and the more fluent his prayers will be.

- *Practice in spontaneous prayer.*

A mealtime blessing need not be a memorized prayer or song. It can be a prayer that your child makes up on his own. Give your child the privilege of breaking away from memorized prayers to pray from his heart at mealtimes. It will be an opportunity for spiritual growth.

- *A time for recognizing that food is a blessing.*

We are exceedingly fortunate in this nation to have sufficient food to eat. Teach your child through mealtime prayers that food is a provision from God and that we must always be thankful to Him for our food and the resulting health, energy, and strength that come from it.

8 ● Pray as You Leave and Enter the House

Peace be to you, peace to your house, and peace to all that you have!

—1 Samuel 25:6

Very few things give a child greater comfort or a feeling of security than knowing that he is safe in his own home, and that his home is a place filled with the peace of the Lord. Strive to make your home such a place.

Peace is a state that comes about when the heavenly Father is invited to dwell within. Make that a part of your child's prayer life.

Heavenly Father, we invite you to live in our home with us. We invite you to live in the heart of each member of our family.

Peace reigns in a home when family members have a relationship marked by forgiveness and forbearance. Make those traits a matter of prayer, too.

Heavenly Father, please help us to forgive one another when we get on each other's nerves or when we hurt one another. Help us to be patient and kind to

*one another. Help us to say 'I'm sorry' and to mean it
when we do something wrong to one another.*

As your children come and go from your peaceful
home, encourage them to pray for two things:

• *Personal protection.*

   A child is often braver in facing life's challenges
when his attention is called to the fact that a safe
haven awaits him at the day's end.

• *Personal blessing.*

   Encourage your child to share with others the presence of the Lord that she experiences in your home.

As you leave your home on vacations, pray that the
Lord will guard your home against intruders until you
return.

For centuries, Jewish people have attached a small
mezuzah to the doorposts of their homes. It is a small
piece of parchment inscribed with passages from Deuteronomy, then rolled and put into a case. The mezuzah
represents the Law to them, which Moses taught them
they were to "write . . . on the doorposts of your
house and on your gates" (Deut. 6:9). As they enter
their homes, the orthodox Jews kiss their fingertips
and then touch the mezuzah. It is a way of acknowledging their arrival into a place sacred to the Lord and set
apart for His presence.

9 • Nothing Is Too Small for Prayer

Are not two sparrows sold for a copper coin? And not one of them falls to the ground apart from your Father's will. But the very hairs of your head are all numbered. Do not fear therefore; you are of more value than many sparrows.

—Matthew 10:29–31

From the time your child begins to understand language, he is told in numerous ways that he is "little." How comforting to a child to know that nothing is too little for God's notice—including little children!

God sees every bird flying in the sky. He knows about every hair on your child's head. And if God knows that, as Jesus Christ taught, then surely God knows when your child:

- *falls off her bicycle;*
- *faces a strange dog in the neighborhood;*
- *rides his skateboard down a hill that is too steep;*
- *has a friend who says something that hurts his feelings;*
- *is excluded from a game.*

Let your child know that he can pray about each accident, mistake, hurt, problem, and embarrassment in his life. God also takes note of:

- *Every kind compliment or word of encouragement your child gives to others;*
- *your child's helpful deeds;*
- *your child's accomplishments and victories; and*
- *every word of praise uttered by your child!*

God is always listening. Indeed, God is eager to hear your child talk to Him about anything and everything.

As you take a walk with your child through a park, make note of the small things that God is seeing, even as you are seeing them.

- Praise Him for the beautiful butterflies that speak to us of God's resurrection power.
- Thank Him for the tiny pebbles in the stream that cause the water to splash and purify itself.
- Notice that it is the leaves of a tree, each one of them quite small, that give life to the tree.
- Watch the insects at work and thank God for the lesson they give, that God has ordered all of creation, with each creature given a specific role and function to fill.

Don't let your children reserve God for big moments, big decisions, or big ceremonies. Create in your child an awareness that God is in every detail and every minute, and that prayer is appropriate for small issues as well as large ones.

10 • Nothing Is Too Big for Prayer

Behold, I am the Lord, the God of all flesh.
Is there anything too hard for Me?
—Jeremiah 32:26

The physical age of a person has very little to do with spiritual capacity or "faith power." Adults may have anemic, underdeveloped, or atrophied faith. Teach your child that he has been given a measure of faith; encourage your child to grow in faith by praying and believing for the hand of God to move on his behalf—even for big miracles!

Danny, a personal family friend, experienced the power of prayer when he was a teenager. While running backwards on a basketball court during a series of drills, Danny fell and broke his arm. An X-ray confirmed the break in the femur. The attending physician told Danny that he would need to put a cast on the arm and that he would not be able to resume his basketball career for at least six weeks. A major game was coming up in two weeks.

Danny's mother, Judy, had been listening to a sermon about healing before the accident happened, and when the doctor left the examining room Danny and Judy began to pray together for a complete and rapid healing of Danny's arm. When the physician returned, Judy and Danny asked that only a soft cast be put on his arm. He reluctantly agreed, with the provision that Danny would return in a day or so and be examined again.

After leaving the doctor's office, Danny and his mother proceeded to a friend's house, where the group read scriptures related to healing, laid hands on Danny and prayed, and partook of Communion together.

Several days passed and the coach kept Danny on the bench during basketball practices. Danny told his coach, "God cares about all of my life, including basketball. He knows how much I want to play and He's healed my arm. I know He has!" Danny returned to the doctor and had a second X-ray. It confirmed what Danny already knew—the break had healed completely. Danny was able to play in the championship game as he had hoped!

"But what if my child doesn't experience a miracle or see an answer from God?" you may ask. "Won't that destroy his faith or cause him to be discouraged in his relationship with God?" No, not if you teach your child one simple but vital fact about prayer. It is *our* responsibility to pray and to believe and to ask God for the desires of our heart. It is *God's* responsibility to answer our prayers according to His wisdom.

We can't do God's part and He won't do ours. Furthermore, God wants us to ask. The prime reason for your child to pray is to give God the opportunity to work as He wills.

11 • Sometimes God Says Yes

So I say to you, ask, and it will be given to you; seek, and you will find; knock, and it will be opened to you.

—Luke 11:9

Some people seem afraid to ask God for things because they fear He will say no. Try taking the opposite approach. Ask God for things because He may very well say yes!

Teach your child that God sees our requests in the total context of our lives. He knows the beginning from the ending. He knows us far better than we know ourselves. He knows our weaknesses and our strengths. He knows what will make us happy and what will make us sad. He knows what is good for us.

Teach your child to pray,

> *God, you know everything about me. You know what is right for me. I want [petition]. If it's OK with You for me to have that, I'd sure like it!*

Assure your child that God only wants what is good for his or her total well-being. Teach your child to pray,

> *Heavenly Father, I want your best for my life. You know what that is. Please send it my way.*

Let your child be bold in asking for what he needs.

Heavenly Father, I ask You to heal me. I ask you to keep me safe . . . to provide enough food and water for me . . . to give me warmth when it's cold and cool shelter when it's hot.

Encourage your child to ask for spiritual blessings.

Heavenly Father, I want to feel more of Your presence. I want to experience Your love for me. I want to be assured You are always there for me. I want Your forgiveness . . . Your guidance . . . Your wisdom . . . Your compassion.

Give your child permission to ask God for things that give him or her pleasure. Teach your child that the heavenly Father experiences joy in what causes us to feel joy!

Encourage your child to ask God for the things he wants, not only for the things he needs. Your child may well discover that God says yes far more than He says no.

12 ● Sometimes God Says No

"For My thoughts are not your thoughts,
Nor are your ways My ways," says the Lord.
"For as the heavens are higher than the
  earth,
So are My ways higher than your ways,
And My thoughts than your thoughts."
—Isaiah 55:9

We don't know all of the reasons that God doesn't answer our prayers with the answers that we want. But we do know some of the reasons, and you can explain these reasons to your child.

- God sees our entire life. He will not give us something now that may lead to harm later in our life, or in eternity.
- God not only sees our lives but the lives of all around us. He will never give us something that might cause harm to someone else.
- God sees our weaknesses. He will not give us something that makes us weaker still.
- Above all, God has a purpose and a reason even when He says no.

Does that mean we should stop asking of God? No! We still have the privilege to ask and we should ask of God.

God's Decision Is Best Shari, a young friend of mine, desperately wanted a part in a movie that was being shot in her city. She prayed about being chosen as a part of the local cast, and she asked others to join with her in prayer. When the day came for auditions, Shari wasn't chosen. She was heartbroken. Frankly, she didn't understand why God had said no to something that she wanted so much and for which she showed so much talent. She was excluded from several social outings as her friends began to form new associations with the "movie people."

As the months passed, Shari began to hear reports about the behavior of her friends who had been chosen for the movie. They were becoming quite rebellious at home and at school. They began experimenting with drugs during the course of the filming, and they began to drink excessively. Shari watched silently as her friends became rowdier and, eventually, even began to break the law.

After about six months, the day came when Shari said to her mother, "I'm glad I wasn't chosen to be in the movie. I'm afraid I might not have been strong enough to withstand the pressure to go along with the rest of the gang. I could be in serious trouble by now."

Shari realized that even though she had experienced hurt initially at God's saying no, God had actually spared her a far greater hurt that could have impacted her entire life.

13 • Sometimes God Says "Not Now"

To everything there is a season,
A time for every purpose under heaven.
—Ecclesiastes 3:1

The Bible has a great deal to say about the "fullness of time," the precise, appropriate moment, from God's perspective, when things should happen for maximum and eternal good. How important it is that we teach our children about the *fullness* of God's time for certain things in their lives. And how difficult it is for children, sometimes, to comprehend that lesson.

One of the best ways I know to convey the concept of "God's perfect timing" is to plant seeds with your child. I suggest you choose beans as a plant to grow since they tend to germinate and produce quickly. Pray with your child as you plant your seeds,

> *Heavenly Father, we ask you to give us beans.*

As the seed comes up, pray again,

> *Heavenly Father, we ask you to give us beans.*

As the leaves began to form and the plant grows tall, pray yet again,

Heavenly Father, we ask you to give us beans.

The day will come when the pods begin to form.

Heavenly Father, we ask you to give us beans.

Finally, the pods will be ready to pick and to open— revealing beans!

Point out to your child that God had *begun* to answer your prayer for beans at the time you first planted the seed. The fullness of the answer, however, was actually realized at the moment when you opened the pod to find beans.

Teach your child that many of our prayers are like that prayer for beans. They are good and right petitions before the throne of God, but we are often praying in advance of God's right moment for answering our prayer fully. What shall we do when God's answer is "not yet" or "not now"? It is at those times that we need to *keep* praying and believing.

Our son Rob had no doubt whatsoever that he would pass his driving test on his sixteenth birthday. He had an ardent interest in hot rods and motorcycles and had quickly mastered the basic skills of driving. He failed, however, to pass the test on his first attempt. Embarrassed and hurt, Rob realized that God had said, "Not now." A few months later, Rob passed the test and with a near-perfect score. However, that experience cooled his interest in cars and cycles. Simultaneously, his love for the Lord began to grow by leaps and bounds, and he developed a new interest—medicine. Today, Rob is a physician and an assistant professor at a medical school where he is actively involved in cancer research and bone marrow transplants. Sometimes God says "not now" in order to divert our attention to His higher purposes for our lives.

In nearly all cases, "not now" answers teach us patience, and as we continue to pray and believe, our faith grows, too.

14 ● Pray Before a Visit to the Doctor, Dentist, or Hospital

You will keep him in perfect peace,
Whose mind is stayed on You,
Because he trusts in You.
—Isaiah 26:3

Is your child fearful of a visit to the doctor or dentist? Pray about that appointment with your child.

Children generally have two fears in this area. The first is that of pain or discomfort. Teach your child to ask for help from the Lord.

> *Help me to be able to stand any pain that may come. Help me to trust You to be able to endure any procedure and to know that any hurt I feel is only going to last a little while. If I need to have a shot, help the nurse to give it to me in the right way so that it won't hurt very much. Help me to be brave. Help me to trust You for my complete healing.*

The second fear is that of the unknown. Perhaps more than any other environment your child experiences, a doctor's or dentist's office is filled with equipment that looks ominous, surfaces that seem cold and hard, and procedures that are foreign. Teach your child to call on the name of the Lord when he feels fear:

Jesus be with me. Jesus help me. Jesus, take away any fear or worry that might try to take over my mind and my heart. Help me to trust You to bring me through this experience victoriously.

Our son Rob faced surgery for torn ligaments when he was a child. As he was wheeled away from us into the surgical theatre, we saw his face turn ashen and terror fill his eyes. The surgeon came to us a few minutes later and said that Rob's blood pressure had soared to a dangerous level.

We asked to speak with Rob briefly. We said, "Honey, just call on the name of the Lord. Call out to Jesus. He'll be with you in this." We heard Rob begin to say, "Jesus . . . Jesus . . . Jesus." He continued to repeat only the name of the Lord, over and over and over. Within a few minutes, a calm came over his entire being, his blood pressure dropped, and he went through the surgery without any further incident.

In times of fear, your child may not be able to think of a prayer. He may not be able to form words or even to think of words. Panic can erase all logic, all language ability, all muscle coordination. Teach your child to say only one word as a prayer: the name of Jesus.

15 • Pray Before the Big Event

Blessed be the Lord,
Because He has heard the voice of my
*   supplications!*
The Lord is my strength and my shield;
My heart trusted in Him, and I am
*   helped;*
Therefore my heart greatly rejoices,
And with my song I will praise Him.
                              —Psalm 28:6–7

Encourage your child to pray each and every time he faces a challenge to his skill, ability, talent, or witness:

* before the big game;
* before the recital;
* before the on-stage debut;
* before the court hearing;
* before the concert.

Before any experience in which your child has a doubt as to his own ability to do his best. Teach your child Philippians 4:13. "I can do all things through Christ who strengthens me." Encourage your child to make that a prayer,

> *Heavenly Father, I trust Your word to me that I can,*
> *I can do all things through Christ who strengthens*
> *me.*

About what specifically can your child pray with confidence?

- For the ability to do his best.

    Lord, You are the One who created me and You are the One who has given me talents and abilities. Help me to do my best so that I might be a good witness for You.

Pray, too, that every other person involved will also give a peak performance.

    Help each one to do his best, that we might play well together as a team.

- For the ability to remember all the plays, all the notes, all the calls, all the steps, all the facts, all the Scriptures that pertain to the moment.

    Lord, I trust You to cause my mind to work the way You created it to work. Help me to think clearly and to be sharp mentally.

- For safety.

    Lord, help us to do this without injury or harm to any person.

In some cases, the potential injury may be emotional.

Help us, Lord, not to embarrass any person or to cause anyone to become hurt emotionally. Protect me, Lord, from doing anything that might cause lasting hurt to my heart.

• For confidence.

Help me, Lord, to overcome my jitters. Don't let me be overcome by nervousness. Let me see this as an opportunity to bring glory to You and to bless others.

• For graciousness in winning or losing.

Help us, Lord, to be good sports whether we win or lose. Help us to show your compassion and loving-kindness to those who have competed against us.

Encourage your child to see that every experience in life is like a thread that the Lord is weaving together into a wonderful piece of fabric. The wins are like the warp; the losses are like the woof. It takes both warp and woof—threads running both ways—to make a strong piece of cloth.

16 • Pray for the Desire to Obey

Remind them to be subject to rulers and authorities, to obey, to be ready for every good work, to speak evil of no one, to be peaceable, gentle, showing humility to all men.
—Titus 3:1–2

Obedience is one of the most important lessons any child ever learns—and one of the toughest. All temptation converges on obedience, doesn't it? We are tempted to disobey what we know to be right in God's eyes.

Encourage your child to pray that the Lord will give him or her a desire to obey, and specifically to obey you as a parent or adult with authority over the child.

> *Lord, help me to want to obey my parents when they tell me to do my homework.*

> *Help me, heavenly Father, to want to avoid the people, places, and things that my parents say are bad for me.*

> *I ask you, Lord Jesus, to help me want to do what is pleasing to You.*

Is your teenager beginning to show signs of rebellion? Pray with him or her about it. I did this with our son when he was about thirteen years old.

Ask Your Child to Pray for You   One night, after a rebellious scene, I confronted my son and heard myself saying, "Please pray for me. I want to be a good mother to you. That's my responsibility before God, to train you up to love and serve Him.

"I know you didn't choose me to be your mother. God chose me for that job. God chose you to be my son and to put us together as a family. Would you pray that God will give me wisdom about what I should say to you and how I should train you? Please ask God to help me. I don't want to aggravate you. I want to do things that will eventually bring you blessing."

Something happened that night. The spirit of rebellion in my son began to dissipate. What deep assurance I felt when, through our tears, my son prayed for me and for his obedience.

Finally, pray for and with your child that your child will always be obedient to what the Lord calls him to do, whether he wants to do it or not. Read the story of young Samuel to your child (1 Sam. 3:1–10). Read the parable of Jesus about cheerful obedience in Matthew 21:28–31. Pray with your child,

Heavenly Father, help me always to say yes when you call and to respond cheerfully and willingly to anything that You ask me to do.

17 • Pray for the Ability to Think Clearly and to Learn

Let this mind be in you which was also in Christ Jesus.

—Philippians 2:5

Paul wrote to his coworker Timothy about the nature we are to have in Christ Jesus. He said, "God has not given us a spirit of fear, but of power and of love and of a sound mind" (2 Tim. 1:7). Luke described the young boy Jesus as increasing in "wisdom and stature, and in favor with God and men" (Luke 2:52).

The goal we must hold out to our children is that they develop a sound mind, one that is able to discern clearly the difference between good and evil and one that is firmly established in the things of God. We must always point our children toward the acquisition of wisdom, the ability to think and reason in any situation the way that Jesus would think and reason.

Toward this end, we can encourage our children to pray, "Cause my mind to think the way You made it, Lord!" Specifically, your child can pray for *the ability to concentrate.*

*Help me, heavenly Father, to be able to shut off every-
thing else but this one topic. Help me to focus all of
my attention on learning this material.*

Your child can also pray for the ability to reason
things through.

*Help me, heavenly Father, to see this issue from Your
perspective. Guide my thoughts, Lord, and don't let
me go astray in my thinking.*

Teach your child that his mind is a gift from, and a
creation of, God and that God intends for us to use our
minds to think good thoughts and to solve problems so
this world can be a better place for all people to live.
Teach your child Philippians 4:8. Turn that verse into a
prayer,

*Help me, Heavenly Father, to see your truth in this
subject matter. Help me to see the noble thing in this
history lesson, to focus on the lovely aspects of this
story, to look for the good report in this science lesson.*

Finally, encourage your child to pray before starting
any new unit of study, lesson, test, or homework assign-
ment:

*Help me to learn this to the best of my ability, to
understand this material and to be able to see how I*

might use it some day. Help me to ask questions when I don't understand. Give my teachers wisdom in teaching this lesson and help them to have patience with me as I learn. Thank you for giving me the opportunity to learn more about Your creation and the principles that You have established for my life.

18 • Pray for the Ability to Know

It is the Spirit who bears witness, because the Spirit is truth.

—1 John 5:6

The Spirit of God cannot lie. He only reveals truth. Encourage your child to ask for truth from the Holy Spirit, that he might have the ability to know what is good, right, and true before God. Ask your child to pray,

Heavenly Father, show me what is good. Help me to create good things by your Holy Spirit.

As your child embarks on a creative project, such as a story, a painting, a musical composition, teach him to pray,

Help me, heavenly Father, to produce something that reflects the beauty and harmony and goodness of Your creation.

Your child faces many decisions every day in his relationships with his peers. This is an excellent prayer for your child to say when he is feeling peer pressure.

Heavenly Father, show me what is right in Your eyes. Help me to discern good from evil, right from wrong. Give me boldness to stand up for what You show me is right.

Is your child struggling with his own emotions—his own desires, his own anger or resentments or bitterness, his own loneliness? Encourage your child to pray that the Lord might show Him the truth about who He is in Christ Jesus.

Heavenly Father, show me what You see when you see me. Reveal to me that my sins have been blotted out when I ask You for forgiveness. Let me feel Your presence when I am lonely. Give me the desire to forgive others so that I might be made more like Jesus every day.

Encourage your child to pray for the ability to remember what he learns that is good, right, and true.

Heavenly Father, help me to remember this lesson always.

When King Jehoshaphat of Israel found himself and his people surrounded by three fierce enemy tribes, he cried out to the Lord in prayer. His prayer is one that every child can and should learn:

We have no power against this great multitude that is coming against us; nor do we know what to do, but our eyes are upon You (2 Chron. 20:12).

What should your child do when he doesn't know what to do? Pray—and ask God for His answer!

19 • Pray for Our Nation's Leaders

Therefore I exhort first of all that supplications, prayers, intercessions, and giving of thanks be made for all men, for kings and all who are in authority, that we may lead a quiet and peaceable life in all godliness and reverence.
—1 Timothy 2:1–2

The Bible states clearly in a number of places that we are to respect those in authority. For example, Exodus 22:28 says that we "shall not revile God, nor curse a ruler of [our] people." The Word of God also teaches us that all authority ultimately comes from God, that He raises up whom He will into positions of power, and that He puts down other leaders according to His divine purposes (Ps. 22:8, Prov. 8:15–16, Daniel 2:20–21.)

Encourage your child to pray for our nation's leaders in a fivefold way:

1. Pray for their salvation.

Heavenly Father, I pray that the leaders of our nation will come to have a deep spiritual relationship with You and that they will learn to hear Your voice as they make important decisions about our nation.

2. Pray that our leaders will make wise decisions.

Heavenly Father, please fill [name] with Your wisdom. Cause him or her to make decisions that are pleasing to You and according to Your divine plan.

3. Pray for the physical and emotional strength of our leaders, and that they might have good health.

Heavenly Father, please keep [name] well and strong physically, mentally, and emotionally. Keep him or her safe and healthy!

4. Pray for the families of our leaders. The stress and strain of leadership takes its toll on the families of a leader.

Heavenly Father, please be with the families of [name]. Keep them well and strong, safe and healthy, and their relationships loving and faithful.

5. We are to pray that the leaders will establish an atmosphere whereby the people of our nation will want to know and follow a "knowledge of the truth."

Heavenly Father, help [names] to live a life that is a good example to the people of our land. Help them to lead us in finding Your answers to the problems that we face. We pray they will make and enforce good laws that are fair to all of the people.

The National Children's Prayer Network* in Washington, D.C. is organized to assist children in Sunday schools and Christian schools across the nation to pray daily for our lawmakers. The children write letters to our nation's leaders to let them know that they are praying for them. You can do this, too.

Praying for the leaders of our nation develops in children an understanding of the responsibility of leadership and challenges them to take their place as they grow to maturity.

---

* To contact the National Children's Prayer Network, you may write Lin Story, P.O. Box 9683, Washington, D.C. 20016.

20 • Pray for the Nations

His name shall endure forever;
His name shall continue as long as the
*   sun.*
And men shall be blessed in Him;
All nations shall call Him blessed.
                                    —Psalm 72:17

As Christians, we acknowledge the Lord as our King. He is "high above all nations" (Ps. 113:4) and "King forever" (Ps. 10:16). He is the King of glory, the Lord strong and mighty (Ps. 24:8). He is the King of kings and the Lord of lords (Rev. 17:14).

God has a world view. We should have one, too. God is vitally concerned about all people in all nations. We should be, too.

Do you have a globe, world map, or an atlas in your home? Use it as a focal point for prayer times with your children. Choose one nation and concentrate your prayer time on it.

• *Pray for the leaders of the nation,* that they might come to know the Lord and that they make decisions that reflect God's wisdom.

   Heavenly Father, help the leaders of this nation to rule in a way that brings honor to Your name.

- *Pray for the Christians in the nation.* Are they being persecuted? Pray for their safety. Pray that the Holy Spirit will bring revival among them and that they will win many of their friends and neighbors to the Lord.

    Heavenly Father, be with my brothers and sisters in Christ who are living in this land. Light a fire in their souls that they might be quick to share the Good News of Your Son, Jesus Christ.

- *Pray for the children in the nation.* Do they have sufficient food and clothing? Is there a war raging in their land? Pray for specific needs. Pray that the children will come to hear about Jesus and to love Him as their Savior and Lord.

    Heavenly Father, take care of the little children in this land. Give them food and water and warmth and friends and a safe place to sleep. Send someone to them to tell them about Jesus.

- *Pray for the missionaries and church leaders at work in that nation.* Pray that the Lord will protect them and give them great courage in proclaiming His Word.

    Heavenly Father, help the pastors and evangelists in this nation to show love to the people and to teach them about Jesus. Keep them safe and well. Give them courage and boldness.

Praying in this manner helps your child to develop an "outward view," a view toward

- evangelism;
- reaching out to others and caring about them no matter their race, color, or culture;
- developing a concern that the practical needs of suffering people be met;
- binding their hearts with fellow Christians around the world.

The Scriptures ask us to pray for the blessing of Israel (Gen. 12:3) and for the peace of Jerusalem (Ps. 11:6–7).

Pray for Jesus to come and rule the world in true peace from Jerusalem as He promises.

In and through prayer, help your child see the world as the Father sees it, as the home of *all* His beloved children.

21 • Pray About Events and News Stories That Touch Your Heart

In all things [Jesus] had to be made like His brethren, that He might be a merciful and faithful High Priest in things pertaining to God . . . for in that He Himself has suffered, being tempted, He is able to aid those who are tempted.

—Hebrews 2:17–18

Turn times of concern into times of prayer.

- Is your child concerned about a story he has heard on a television newscast?
- Have you witnessed an accident on the freeway?
- Has a tragedy of some type occurred at your child's school?
- Does your child ask questions about the faces of the children he sees on the milk carton?

Establish a pattern for your child of taking *all* needs of others to the Lord in prayer. The needs may be remote or close to home, big or little. They may be physical, spiritual, material, or emotional in nature.

Perhaps your child has just heard a radio or television report of a major earthquake in a faraway place. He is concerned about it. Channel his concern for others into prayer for them.

> *Heavenly Father, please be with the people who have lost their homes and their loved ones. Comfort their hearts. Give them strength to get through this difficult time. Provide a safe place for them to go. Help them not to be afraid.*

Lindy and Jill, acquaintances of mine, recently asked their mother if they could pray for the missing children whose faces appear on the milk cartons they use every morning as they eat their cereal. They now include their names in their breakfast mealtime prayer:

> *Heavenly Father, help these children* (whom they list by name) *to be found so they can go home to their mothers and fathers. Keep them safe and comfort the hearts of their parents.*

If your child expresses concern after hearing a report about a terrorist bombing, ask your child what Jesus would do. "I think he would heal the people who got hurt and that He'd make sure the people who did this were caught so they couldn't do it again." Pray along those lines.

Heavenly Father, please heal the people who have been injured. Take away the fear in their minds and heal the wounds of their bodies. We ask that You help the police capture the people who set off this bomb.

Encouraging your child to pray as she hears or sees news events that trouble her takes your child's focus off herself and her own fear. It also turns your child's aimless feelings of helplessness into a productive expression that points toward God and toward healing and wholeness.

22 • Pray for the Needy People in Your City

When he flees to one of those cities, and stands at the entrance of the gate of the city, and declares his case in the hearing of the elders of that city, they shall take him into the city as one of them, and give him a place, that he may dwell among them.
—Joshua 20:4

Nearly every child in our nation today will, at some time, encounter a destitute person, someone living in despair. It may be a person or family that comes to your church to receive a meal or a sack of groceries. It may be a person or group of people your child sees as you walk or drive the streets of your city. It may be a report your child sees on television.

Very few thoughts are scarier to a child than the thought that he might not have a home—a bed to call his own, a closet in which to hang his clothes, a place to play and feel safe from the world. What can your child do in confronting his own fears and in expressing concern for the homeless? He can pray!

Homeless people aren't the only people who live in a state of despair. Many people who have homes and jobs still can barely make ends meet financially. Their life is a daily struggle for minimal levels of food, shelter, and clothing. Other families face serious, terminal, or pro-tracted health problems.

When your child encounters a needy person, en-courage your child to pray,

> *Heavenly Father, keep this person safe tonight. Give him a secure place to sleep and people around him who will speak a kind word.*

Encourage your child to pray,

> *Heavenly Father, help my friend who is going through this illness. Ease the suffering. Take away the pain. Heal my friend's body. Don't let my friend become discouraged or depressed. Give my friend Your joy and comfort his family.*

Praying for others who are in need helps children develop an unselfish and compassionate attitude. It keeps pride from their hearts and causes them to be more sensitive to those who are in trouble.

23 • Pray for Friends and Neighbors "To Be in Heaven with Us"

For God so loved the world that He gave His only begotten Son, that whoever believes in Him should not perish but have everlasting life.

—John 3:16

Help your child develop a deep compassion for the eternal souls of others. Join your child in praying that your child's friends will come to have a personal relationship with the Lord Jesus.

When our daughter LeeAnn was in second grade, she said to me one day after she came home from school, "My friend Linda needs to come home with me after school tomorrow."

"Well, LeeAnn," I reminded her, "that's just not going to be possible. We already have other plans." On the verge of tears she responded, "You don't understand, mother, she's *got* to come over *tomorrow.*"

"Why?" I asked. "Why can't she come later in the week?"

"Because she wants to invite Jesus into her heart, and you have to help her do that. She doesn't want to wait any longer."

LeeAnn was right—those other plans could wait! Linda came over the next afternoon and the three of us prayed together that she would have a personal relationship with the Lord Jesus.

Encourage your child to pray,

> *Heavenly Father, help my friends to come to know You and to love You before they die so we can live together in heaven with You and each other forever.*

Let your child know that it's OK for him to pray with his friends.

> *Heavenly Father, my friend wants to know You like I do. I ask You to forgive my friend for his sins and to give him a clean heart. I ask You to send the Holy Spirit to live inside him and to help him to live in a way that is pleasing to you. Help my friend to love You every day of his life, to talk to You often, and to read the Bible so he can learn more about You. I ask You to do this in the name of Jesus.*

When your child prays for the eternal soul of a friend, she develops a compassion for that friend. She learns what it means to love another person as a spiritual "brother" or "sister."

24 • Pray for the Pastor, Sunday School Teacher, and Other Church Leaders

I would not stretch out my hand against the Lord's anointed. And indeed, as your life was valued much this day in my eyes, so let my life be valued much in the eyes of the Lord, and let Him deliver me out of all tribulation.

—1 Samuel 26:23–24

Tell your child the story about Moses, Aaron, and Hur as the Israelites fought against Amalek (Exod. 17:10–13).

As long as Moses held up his hand, Israel prevailed in the battle. When he let down his hand, the enemy Amalek began to win. The Bible says that Moses' hands became "heavy" and he could no longer hold them up. Aaron and Hur "supported his hands, one on one side, and the other on the other side; and his hands were steady until the going down of the sun" (Exod. 17:12). The Israelites won the battle that day.

As a part of the church, your child can help "lift up the hands" of those in leadership by praying for them.

- Pray that they will continue to be strong and well in body, mind, and spirit.

  Heavenly Father, keep my pastor and my Sunday school teacher and all those who lead our church in good health. Keep them strong and well in every area of their lives.

- Pray that they will experience the joy of the Lord every day.

  Heavenly Father, fill my pastor and my Sunday school teacher with Your presence and give them joy in their hearts. Help them to see that their work is important and that they are going to be rewarded by You for all of the good work that they do.

- Pray that they will grow in their ability to teach and to lead.

  Heavenly Father, help my pastor and my Sunday school teacher understand Your Word more every day. Help them to teach us Your Word so that we can understand it, too. Help my pastor follow Your leading and make right decisions for the church.

- Pray that they will have a growing love for all of the people in the church.

  Heavenly Father, help my pastor and Sunday school teacher be kind to every person in our church, to treat everybody with fairness and love, and to be patient with all of us children.

- Pray they will be true to the Word of the Lord always.

  Heavenly Father, keep my pastor and Sunday school teacher from falling into any kind of error or sin. Give them the courage not only to know Your will, but to do it every day of their lives.

Your child's relationship with those in spiritual leadership positions is an important one. Let the relationship be bathed in prayer.

25 • Pray for Family Members

Confess your trespasses to one another, and pray for one another, that you may be healed. The effective, fervent prayer of a righteous man avails much.

—James 5:16

Encourage your child to pray for you, your spouse, his brothers and sisters, and other relatives and family friends. Call them by name. Remember them and their needs before the Lord.

You may want to have a family prayer list that you consult regularly, perhaps keeping it in your family Bible and referring to it for a time of prayer as part of your daily Bible-reading schedule.

Encourage your child to pray for:

• Health and safety.

> *Heavenly Father, I ask You to keep each member of my family strong and well. Keep them from accidents and any kind of harm.*

• Parents to love each other.

Heavenly Father, I ask You to help my mother and daddy love each other, to be kind to one another, and to help each other in every way they can.

• Parents to know what's right to do.

Heavenly Father, I ask You to help my mother and daddy to do what is right for me. Help them to be patient with me and to make good decisions about my life. Help them to understand me and to show their love for me in ways that I can receive it.

• For problems the family member is facing.

Heavenly Father, help my loved one. Show him Your solution for this problem, Your way out of this difficulty, Your provision for this need.

Ask your child to pray for you when you are sick, discouraged about something, facing a problem. Receive your child's prayers! Thank your child for praying for you. When you are well again or the problem has been resolved, let your child know that his prayers have been answered. Praise God together for answered prayer.

• Have your children been fighting all morning? Call them together for a time of prayer. Ask them to pray one for the other.

- Has it been one of those days when all of the family members seemed to be running in circles? Call the family together for prayer. Let every person voice his petition to Father God.
- Has it been a week when nothing in your family life seemed to go according to your plans? Pray together as a family. Give each child an opportunity to pray.

26 • Pray for Teachers and the School Principal

So teach us . . . that we may gain a heart for wisdom.

—Psalm 90:12

Encourage your child to pray frequently for his teachers and those in leadership positions at his school—the principal, the dean, the coach, and so forth. Have your child pray that those who teach him will have:

- Wisdom in teaching. Teaching requires more than knowledge; it requires an ability to convey that knowledge so that it is received, understood, applied, and valued.

   Heavenly Father, please give my teacher Your wisdom. Let my teacher see clearly what it is that is most important for me to know. Help her to know how to keep discipline in the classroom.

- An ability to communicate.

   Heavenly Father, help my teacher to explain things

thoroughly and to give clear instructions. Help me to understand what my teacher says.

• Fairness.

Heavenly Father, help my teacher treat us all fairly. Don't let my teacher have special "pets." Help my teacher give us each an opportunity to do our best.

• Patience.

Heavenly Father, help my teacher to be patient with me and with all of the children in my class. Give her a good sense of humor, Lord. Help her to be gentle in her discipline.

• A soft heart for God.

Heavenly Father, help my teacher to grow in his relationship with You. Keep his heart tender toward Your Spirit and toward Your leading. Don't let him criticize the things of God or the people of God.

Has your child disobeyed a teacher and been punished for it? Encourage your child to pray for forgiveness and a restoration of his relationship with the teacher.

Heavenly Father, I'm sorry for what I did at school today. Please forgive me. Help my teacher not to hold this against me in the future. Please heal my relationship with my teacher.

Make certain that your child's prayers for his or her teacher, and others in positions of school leadership, are kept positive and uplifting. Join your child in these prayers. Send a message to your child that you, the teacher, and the child are a team that is working together for your child's good.

27 • Pray Any Time and Anywhere

Help me, O Lord my God!
Oh, save me according to Your mercy,
That they may know that this is Your
*   hand—*
That You, LORD, have done it!
*   —Psalm 109:26–27*

Let your child know that it is 100 percent permissible to pray any time and anywhere. He can pray:

- alone or with others;
- softly to himself or aloud;
- long or short.
- No matter what!

Let your child know that he doesn't need to postpone his prayers until the next visit to church, or even wait until the family prayer time before he goes to bed. He can pray at the time a need occurs. God has an open-door policy night and day.

Assure your child that any place on the earth can become a prayer room.

- Daniel prayed in a den filled with hungry lions.
- Shadrach, Meshach, and Abed-Nego prayed in a burning, fiery furnace, even as an angry king and people watched.

- Peter cried out in prayer as he began to sink after walking on the waters of the Sea of Galilee, with all of the other disciples watching from the boat.
- Paul and Silas prayed and sang praises in a jail cell.

Our daughter LeeAnn turned the corral of a Montana ranch into a prayer room one afternoon as she was taming an appaloosa horse. We came to the corral railings to hear her calling out to the Lord for help and safety, completely oblivious to any around her.

Assure your child that our Father God always hears your child's prayer and will act on her behalf. That's what Jesus showed us when He stopped on a trip through Jericho to heal a blind man named Bartimaeus, when He stopped on His way to Jairus's house to heal a woman who reached out to touch the hem of His garment, when He interrupted His own sermon to heal a man with a withered hand, and when he postponed a prayer retreat to talk to little children.

Let your child know that prayer is a time of direct communication between your child and God.

28 ● Pray in Times of Personal Emergency

Save now, I pray, O Lord.
—Psalm 118:25

Prayers do not need to be flowery, long, or stated grammatically to be heard, understood, and acted upon by Father God. Assure your child of that fact. God hears SOS prayers. The Scriptures are filled with examples:

- Jonah, in the belly of a great fish;
- Paul, in a storm at sea;
- Esther, as she faced a death sentence along with her people.

God hears and answers our cries for help.

When I was a child, I was riding my bicycle one day when I was confronted by a large, mean, and very fast-running dog. At least, that is the way I remember that dog. The more I tried to talk reasonably to the dog, the louder it barked. The faster I pedaled my bicycle, the faster it ran, nipping at my heels on the pedals. Finally, I called out to God in desperation, "Lord, I need help *now!*" Immediately, the dog stopped in his tracks, ceased barking, and when I finally turned around to see what had happened, he was calmly walking back home.

"Lord, I need help *now*" is a simple prayer that any child can learn, even at a very young age. The prayer actually has four important lessons in it for your child.

- *Lord.* Your child is calling on the Lord for help, not upon any other person, organization, or thing. The Lord should always be your child's first line of thought in times of trouble or emergency.
- *I need.* It is important for your child to recognize his dependency upon the Lord, and the fact that he has needs that only the Lord can meet. Nobody is completely self-sufficient. Acknowledging need is an important step for your child to take in his spiritual growth.
- *Help.* The Lord's help comes in many different forms. Sometimes it's a deliverance from a mean dog. Sometimes it's deliverance from mean people. Sometimes it's deliverance from circumstances, sickness, the threat of death, an impending accident. Sometimes it's deliverance from the influence of evil powers. The Lord's ability to help is not limited. It is available around the clock.
- *Now.* The Lord God is always in the "now" moments of our lives. He is not slow to act or reluctant to act. Very often a child's prayers for "now" help are answered with immediacy.

This prayer is ultimately a prayer of utter dependence upon the Lord to do what only He can do in our lives—deliver us from evil.

29 • Pray That God Will Change Things

We know that all things work together for good to those who love God, to those who are the called according to His purpose.
—Romans 8:28

Our privilege as sons and daughters of God—no matter our physical ages—is to ask God to deliver us from any form of evil and to cause circumstances to change for our good.

We experienced this in a powerful way when our children were young teenagers. New neighbors moved in across the street from us, and shortly thereafter problems began to surface, mostly involving their two older teenage sons. The neighbor boys freely consumed alcohol and used drugs as they worked on their cars in the driveway. The more we tried to befriend the family, the worse the problems seemed to grow.

The boys played loud music from midafternoon until late at night and all weekend long. One day as I was gardening with the children, we noticed that the earth was shaking under our knees from the vibrations of the music being played down the hill and across the street. We began to pray there in the yard.

Heavenly Father, we feel as if we are living under the influence of evil, and we ask you to deliver us from it. We ask you to deliver these teenage boys across the street from sin and to bring them into a salvation experience with You or to remove them from this neighborhood. Thank you, Lord Jesus, for being our Deliverer.

The children also prayed,

Heavenly Father, we ask that the family that comes to live in this house would be a Christian family. Please, Lord, send a family with a boy and a girl so we can have Christian playmates.

The Lord answered the prayers exactly. Two months later, the family was transferred to another city. A lovely Christian family moved into the house within a few days, and they had a son and a daughter for our children to play with.

Encourage your child to pray for deliverance from evil and for the establishment of good.

• It may be a prayer that another child at school will stop his bullying, or her arguing, or his pestering, or her teasing.
• It may be a prayer that pornographic materials will be removed from a neighborhood quick-stop store.
• It may be a prayer that a mean or noisome animal in

the neighborhood will be given a new home (away from yours).

At some point in your child's life, he or she will undoubtedly be confronted by evil. Arm your child in advance with three prayers: one for deliverance, another for God's best provision, and one for the courage to run away from evil.

30 • Thank God for Good Things When They Come

Thanks be to God for His indescribable gift!
—2 Corinthians 9:15

Every perfect gift in our lives ultimately comes from God, our loving Provider:

- each day of your child's life and every hour in it;
- each meal;
- each breath he takes, each beat of his heart;
- each word of encouragement, hug, or kiss from a loving parent;
- each toy or gift item she receives;
- each opportunity and challenge to grow;
- each bit of information, insight, and revelation;
- each friend and loved one;
- *everything!*

Encourage your child to honor God as the Source of all good things in his life and to honor God as the supreme Gift-giver. Encourage your child to offer a prayer of thanks any time she experiences something good.

Four-year-old Catherine prayed this bedtime prayer as she lay in her aunt's king-sized bed one evening during an overnight stay: "Thank you, Lord, that we got to eat pizza tonight. Thank you, Lord, that I get to spend the night with my aunt and sleep in this big bed." She said with great gusto, "And *thank you,* God, that I get to eat cereal for breakfast!"

No item is too small to be worthy of thanks. No gift is too small. No treat is too trivial.

Our two-year-old grandson Joshua is a living bundle of enthusiasm. Nothing seems too small for his exuberant acknowledgement. This past Christmas he came to me after we had all exchanged presents and said with great excitement, "Aren't you *glad* you got that present?" I sense a great future ahead for him as a child of praise!

Encourage your child to memorize James 1:17. "Every good gift and every perfect gift is from above, and comes down from the Father of lights, with whom there is no variation or shadow of turning."

- Prayers of thanksgiving focus the attention of your child on what he has, not on what he doesn't have.
- Prayers of thanksgiving help your child develop a grateful heart.
- Prayers of thanksgiving turn your child's attention to God as the Giver behind every gift, and lessens his reliance on people for those things that bring true joy into our lives.

31 • Praise God for the Things He Has Made

In the beginning God created the heavens and the earth.

—Genesis 1:1

Acknowledge God as the Creator of all things! Teach your child to praise Him for His creation:

- For stars that fill the sky and the moon that glows so brilliantly, changing its shape by degrees each night.
- For bubbling streams and mighty ocean waves and wispy waterfalls and clear mountain lakes.
- For cool sand and polished rocks and shells that wash up on the seashore.
- For the animals of the forest, jungle, and desert. For the animals in your neighborhood. For your child's pet.
- For nutritious food and clean water to drink.

All of nature is a living panorama of God's goodness. Take a nature walk with your child and turn it into a praise service. Let your child offer praise for each item he sees:

Praise God for the caterpillar. Praise God for the leaf.
Praise God for the tree. Thank you, God, for making
these things. They give me pleasure. They teach me
lessons. Thank you for the gift they are to me!

Praising God for His creation helps to establish two
principles in your child's life. First, God is the Creator.
Every aspect of His creation is "original" and "special."
What God has created, He knows how to sustain,
mend, heal, and cause to grow and multiply.

All life-giving acts and manifestations of creativity ultimately come from God. Teach your child to praise
Him,

I thank You and praise You, O God, for all of Your
handiwork. Thank You for making me. Thank You
for taking care of me and for making me a one-of-a-
kind original.

Second, God has a purpose for every aspect of His
creation, including the life of your child. Teach your
child to praise Him,

I thank You and praise You, O God, for the way in
which You have created me. Thank You for the tal-
ents, abilities, skills, and opportunities You have
given me. Cause me to bloom where You have
planted me.

32 • Tell God Exactly How You Feel

I am weary with my groaning;
All night I make my bed swim;
I drench my couch with my tears.
My eye wastes away because of grief;
It grows old because of all my enemies.
—Psalm 6:6–7

Give your child the assurance that God is never going to be shocked or surprised by what your child says to Him. Let your child know that he can be totally honest with God and express anything that is on his heart.

Your child can tell God when he is

• **Wondering about life.** God delights in hearing your child's questions. He will find a way to answer them. A little friend of mine was once overheard asking the Lord in prayer,

> *And God, I've been wondering—do caterpillars like cottage cheese?*

• **Troubled or concerned.** Children are capable of worry. Children can get ulcers, too. Through prayer, your child experiences the peace of God.

Help me not to be afraid, God, of what the future holds. Fill my heart with Your peace.

- **Angry.** Better to pray than to pout! Anger dissipates as your child prays and trusts the situation to God.

  I'm angry and upset about this, God. Free me from this feeling of anger as I trust You to take care of this situation.

- **Happy.** God wants to know how happy your child is when he wins a victory, or receives a nice compliment, or does well at something he's attempted. God delights in your child's successes as much as you do as a parent.

  Heavenly Father, thank you for the good thing that happened to me today. I know You planned it just for me!

- **Sad.** Does your child carry a deep burden of sorrow? Has she been rejected? Is she discouraged at repeated failures? Encourage her to turn to the Lord in prayer and to express just how she feels to the Lord.

  Heavenly Father, this situation makes me so sad I just want to cry all the time. Please bind up my broken heart and take away this ache that I feel. Show me things I can do to make this situation better.

Teach your child that she can trust God with things that she wouldn't even tell her best friend. God can and will keep your child's secret, He can and will forgive any sin your child confesses to Him, He can and will act on your child's behalf.

Prayer about feelings helps your child develop a truly "conversational" relationship with the Lord. Your child will come to know what it means to "walk with Him, and talk with Him" on a daily basis.

33 • Pray for the Ability to Forgive Others (Who Hurt You Unintentionally)

Whenever you stand praying, if you have anything against anyone, forgive him, that your Father in heaven may also forgive you your trespasses. But if you do not forgive, neither will your Father in heaven forgive your trespasses.

—Mark 11:25

Children are beginners when it comes to interpreting human behavior and the actions of others. We adults sometimes forget that fact. Children often take the words and actions of others far more personally or more deeply than is intended by the other party.

Prayer helps to heal the injured emotions and feelings of rejection that children feel when they are unintentionally excluded from games or parties, overlooked by teachers, punished unfairly, left out of a secret, or ignored by someone with whom they would like to be friends.

• Encourage your child to pray,

Heavenly Father, hold my heart in Your hand so that no matter what others may do to me, I will feel Your warmth of security, and love.

• Encourage your child to admit how he feels in prayer and to ask the Lord to resolve any negative feelings he harbors toward others.

Heavenly Father, my feelings were hurt today by what my friend said. Help me not to feel so bad. Help me to forgive my friend in my heart.

• Encourage your child to ask God to give him an understanding of why other people act the way they do.

Heavenly Father, help me to understand why my friend did what she did. Help me to see my friend as You do. Help me to love her and to be patient with her.

• Encourage your child to ask for restraint not to strike back.

Heavenly Father, help me to forget what happened and to get over this desire I have to strike back and get even.

When your child forgives others he opens up the

door to receive forgiveness in his own life. Forgiving others is the key to a life uncluttered by bitterness and resentment, which develop into meanness. Encourage your child to forgive freely!

34 • Pray for Those Who Persecute You (Intentionally)

Love your enemies, bless those who curse you, do good to those who hate you, and pray for those who spitefully use you and persecute you, that you may be sons of your Father in heaven.

—Matthew 5:44–45

Persecution is intentional. It is often premeditated. It may come because your child is standing up for what is right in God's eyes. Unfortunately, your child will probably experience it at some time during his childhood. He may be persecuted by:

- the class bully,
- the older child down the street,
- the ringleader of the gang,
- the rebel, or
- the relentless tease.

We all know such children and we all know that they seem to have no capacity for mercy. Sometimes the persecution comes in the form of ridicule. It may be manifested as rejection. It may come in the form of teasing.

As you teach your child to pray for those who are persecuting her, teach your child that Jesus, who hears your child's prayer, knows what it means to be persecuted. He was persecuted to the point of death! He understands how your child feels.

> *Thank you, Jesus, for knowing how I feel when other people persecute me. Help me to be able to take whatever they dish out and to respond as You would.*

Encourage your child to ask the Lord for wisdom about how to respond to persecution.

> *Please show me, heavenly Father, what I should do. How should I talk to this person? Should I ignore him? Should I try to be friends with him? What is the right thing to say?*

Turning the other cheek, facing persecution, praying for those who hurt you are all tough things to do at any age. What a valuable reward is promised, however, to those who do. They will be called the sons and daughters of God.

35 • Thank God for Sending Jesus

The next day John saw Jesus coming toward him, and said, "Behold! The Lamb of God who takes away the sin of the world!
—John 1:29

"Why did Jesus come to the earth?" That's a good question to discuss with your children. Explain to your child that Jesus came to show us what God is like and to show us how to live in a way that is pleasing to God. Talk about incidents in the life of Jesus that reveal various traits of God, that show us how to respond in certain situations, and that show the love of God extended toward us.

Jesus showed us that God:

- *Wants us to be whole in body, mind, spirit, and emotions.* Time and again, Jesus said to people, "Be thou made whole." Encourage your child to ask God for wholeness.

    Heavenly Father, please make me whole. You know the parts of my life where I am weak or unable to do certain things. Please give me Your strength in those areas. Make me whole.

- *Wants us to live with Him forever.* That is the very reason that Jesus died on the Cross. He became the supreme sacrifice for sin so that we won't have to die for our sins.

Heavenly Father, thank you that you want me to live with You always in Heaven.

This fact truly hit home to a dear family friend, Amy, when she was with us one year at the Garden Tomb in Jerusalem. It was Amy's first visit to Israel, and as she walked out of the empty tomb she was deeply moved. "He's really alive!" she said.

- *Wants us to love one another.* Jesus continually taught that it was God's desire that we love one another, do good one to another, pray for one another, and build one another up so that we can all grow to be more like Him.

  Help me, heavenly Father, to grow up to think and talk and act like Jesus, Your Son. I want to be more and more like Him—and like You—every day.

Encourage your child to thank God for sending Jesus every time he hears a Bible story about Jesus, and every time he has a new spiritual insight into the life of the Lord. Encourage your child to thank Him for the lessons that He continues to teach us day by day as we obey His Word.

36 • Include Your Child in Prayer Meetings

Jesus said, "Let the little children come to Me, and do not forbid them; for of such is the kingdom of heaven.

—Matthew 19:14

Include your child in your prayer meetings and church services. Don't send him away to another room to play or to be entertained. Don't exclude her from the presence of the Lord. That's what Jesus's disciples tried to do to the children one day and Jesus soundly rebuked them. "Let them come," said Jesus. "Don't forbid them. Give them the opportunity to be in My presence and to experience who I am!"

Children learn by watching others and then copying them. Let your child learn how to pray by watching you pray. Give your child an opportunity to experiment and to "try out" prayer.

Your child may not feel much boldness in the Lord. Your child may not feel like saying anything. Still, allow your child the freedom to be a part of your prayer meeting and to pray to the extent that he or she *wants* to pray.

Often, children are just comfortable "being" in a room where prayer is happening. In fact, they may relax so much that they go to sleep. Let that happen! Our grandchildren have been in three-hour home prayer meetings all their lives. They're entirely comfortable sitting for a while, climbing up on the lap of this one and that one, lying on the floor, sometimes praying, sometimes watching, sometimes dozing. Give your child the freedom to move around during a prayer meeting, to shift positions, to stand for a while, and to sit for a while. Let her relax in the Lord's presence and feel comfortable, yet reverent, in His throne-room.

Tell your child in advance what you expect of him during the meeting. Let him know the limits you will place on his behavior before the meeting begins.

The Bible does not prescribe a set position for prayer. Some people in the Bible prayed standing up, others were prostrate on their faces before God. Some kneeled; some prayed as they walked; some lifted up holy hands. Give your child the freedom of position that Bible people enjoyed. Let your child stand or sit or move about as he prays.

You can help train your child to take part in group prayer meetings. Give your child the freedom to add an "amen" to any other person's prayer with which he agrees. Or ask him to pray just one word of thanksgiving during a family prayer meeting, a word such as *safety* or *friends*. Move, next, to one sentence from each person in your family or small-group prayer meeting.

Thank you that I got to play with Jenny today.

Thank you that we got to have pizza for dinner.

Let the children come. Jesus did.

37 ● Pray Aloud

Jesus lifted up His eyes and said, "Father, I thank You that You have heard Me."
—John 11:41

Prayer is *voicing* our petitions to the Lord. Praise is *declaring* the wonderful and mighty deeds of the Lord to the earth.

Petitioning is asking things of God. This is the way that God chose for us to communicate with Him, so that in His love, He can answer our requests.

When we pray silently, our prayer is heard in heaven and recorded there as all of our thoughts are. But, when we want something done on earth, we should ask aloud with all our heart. Teach your child to pray aloud.

Two things happen when a person prays aloud. First, the person who is praying is also listening. He is hearing his own voice. He's hearing his own petitions. Second, very often we don't really know what we think about a matter until we start talking about it. Sometimes we are surprised at what comes out of our own mouths. That happens in prayer, too. The Holy Spirit guides our prayer and leads us to pray in ways that we may not have initially thought or planned to pray.

Jesus said, "Whatever you *ask* in prayer, believing, you will receive" (Matt. 21:22). Ask verbally. Teach your child to voice his concerns, to speak out of his feelings, to lift up his voice in praise to God.

From the time our children were born again (during

their elementary school years), I wouldn't let more than three days go by without hearing them pray. I'd let them get by with silent prayers or "I don't want to pray" responses for no longer than three days, and then I canceled all my plans, and theirs. We would spend a delightful time together talking about the wonderful ways of Jesus. By the time evening had come, their personal relationship with the Lord was renewed so that they would again be eager to pray aloud. I knew if they went longer than three days, something was amiss in their lives—their prayers were a barometer of their relationship with the Lord. If a child is in the habit of praying aloud, his sudden refusal to pray aloud can be a clear indication of a problem he is experiencing or of something that is troubling him spiritually.

Insist that your child pray aloud. Pray aloud in your child's presence. In so doing, you'll reveal your souls to one another and enter into new levels of communication that are the richest and dearest you'll ever know.

38 • Pray During the Storms of Life

O Lord God of hosts,
Who is mighty like You, O Lord?
Your faithfulness also surrounds You.
You rule the raging of the sea;
When its waves rise, You still them.
—Psalm 89:8–9

You do not need to stop what you are doing in order to pray. Pray as you do, pray as you go, pray as you move.

This is an important lesson to teach your children when they feel threatened by powerful forces coming against them. Panic paralyzes. Prayer frees.

When our children were in junior high, a raging fire threatened the neighborhood where we lived. The weather had been extremely dry and the grasses were just like tinder in both of the canyons on either side of our house. When fire broke out, it spread quickly, burning many houses in its path.

One of my most vivid scenes of this entire afternoon was seeing my daughter LeeAnn running for water, her arms waving an empty water bucket and praying loudly against the fire as it moved ever closer to the neighbors' yard. Bucket after bucket after bucket of water was carried in prayer, all of us beseeching the Lord to stop the fire before it damaged the home of our neighbors, fellow Christians.

The winds changed direction that afternoon, blowing the fire back into itself. Although the grasses had charred themselves all the way to our neighbors' fence, their yard had no damage. The fire did not cross the road. Our property was spared. We felt as David must have felt when he declared in song, "He is my refuge and my fortress;/My God, in Him I will trust./Surely He shall deliver you from the snare of the fowler/And from the perilous pestilence" (Ps. 91:2–3).

- When lightning flashes and the thunder rolls, pray even as you take refuge from the storm!
- When the ship tosses on the storm sea, pray even as you batten down the hatches and tighten your life vest!
- When the hurricane blows with its fury toward your home, pray even as you board up the windows!

No matter what the terror that is lashing out at you— pray!

O God, save us now! Hosanna! *

---

* *Hosanna* is actually a prayer which means "Lord, save us now."

39 • Pray in Times of Death

Now may our Lord Jesus Christ Himself, and our God and Father, who has loved us and given us everlasting consolation and good hope by grace, comfort your hearts and establish you in every good word and work.

—2 Thessalonians 2:16–17

Death is a part of life, even the lives of many children. Grieving and sorrow are a part of death, and thus, of life. Prayer can bring healing for the grief-stricken heart of a child.

• Talk about heaven and eternity with your child. Describe heaven in concrete terms. Anticipate what life in heaven will be like. Pray to live so that you will go to heaven when you die.

> *Thank you, heavenly Father, that I can live with You someday in heaven. You are the Giver of Life and have all control over death. I look forward to being with You in that safe, happy place You are preparing for me.*

• Assure your child that it's OK to feel sad and to cry. Even Jesus cried at the tomb of his friend Lazarus.

*Heavenly Father, You see my heart and You know
how sad I am that I can't be with this person that I
love. Please heal this ache in my heart.*

• Assure your child of God's protection over his life.
When he feels weak and vulnerable, turn his
thoughts to prayer.

*Heavenly Father, thank You that You are always
there. Please provide everything that we need—the
money to pay our bills, a place to live, enough food to
eat. I trust You to take care of us.*

• Discuss with your child the unfathomable wisdom of
God. There is no understanding the why's of death.
God has a reason that we don't know and can't know
in the midst of our grief.

*Heavenly Father, we can't begin to know all of Your
reasons for the things that happen to us, including
the time of our death. Help us to accept the fact of this
loved one's death as part of Your wisdom and love.
We trust You with our life and with our death.*

40 • Pray for Help in the New Place

Do not fear, little flock, for it is your Father's good pleasure to give you the kingdom.

—Luke 12:32

Your child may face a number of new situations, new challenges, new environments as he grows up:

- the new house and neighborhood;
- the first trip to camp;
- the new school or teacher;
- the new church and Sunday school class; or
- the first part-time job.

Prayer can help ease the transition from the old and familiar to the new and scary.

Pray for and with your child to have courage. Give your child some people-meeting skills. Encourage your child to make the first move, "Hi, my name is [name]. What's yours?" Prepare your child with some conversation-starting questions.

Thank you, heavenly Father, for going with me into this new setting. I trust You to be by my side and to help me to look people right in the eye and introduce myself and to not be scared.

Pray for and with your child to be a giver in the new setting. Express to your child how much he has to offer to the new situation or setting. Encourage your child to look for opportunities to give to others in the new setting.

Heavenly Father, help me to be brave as I meet new people. Help me to see ways in which I can help them. They may be just as scared as I am. Help me to be a friend to them.

Pray that your child will be alert in his new surroundings. A new environment or setting can sometimes be so overwhelming that it "freezes" a child. Prepare your child as much as you can in advance of the day when she goes into the new setting by telling her as much as you know about the new school, the camp, the job, the neighborhood. Give your child as much advance information as you can.

Heavenly Father, help me to see everything that is interesting and beautiful in this new place. Don't let me be so scared that I become afraid to explore.

As your child leaves you to embark on his journey into the unknown setting, pray even as you hug him goodbye,

Thank you, Lord Jesus, that You are going with my child and that You will be with him every second of this day and every day in this place. Help him to do his best and to be a witness for You.

Assure your child that Jesus understands what it's like to face a new situation or enter a new place. After all, as just a toddler, he moved to a foreign land, and then a few years later, moved again to a place he didn't know. He encountered new people and new situations His entire life.

Thank you, Lord Jesus, that You know exactly what I'm facing and how I'm feeling because You've felt this way, too.

Give your child directions about how he can get back home to you. It may be via a quarter and a phone number tucked into a pocket. It may be a little map that he helps to prepare. Assure your child that he can reach you in an emergency. At the same time, assure your child that he is never out of the heavenly Father's sight.

Thank you, heavenly Father, that You know all about this new place and You are there with me always!

41 • Pray for Courage to Stand Up to Peer Pressure

Behave courageously, and the Lord will be with the good.

—2 Chronicles 19:11

Your child is going to face temptation. It may be:

- smoking,
- drinking,
- using drugs,
- looking at pornographic magazines,
- telling dirty jokes,
- going to a bad movie,
- engaging in sexual activities,
- watching a horror video,
- shoplifting,
- any other form of sin.

Prepare your child in advance. Turn the popular just-say-no campaign slogan into a prayer:

Lord, help me to say no!

Children need to be taught that they have both the authority and the ability to say "No" to any form of evil, temptation, or lie. They do not need to play along, play dumb, or play with fire.

Children have the *authority* to say no because the One whom they are ultimately trying to please is their heavenly Father. Friends are fun to have. It's nice to be noticed and included by peers. But their standards may not be God's.

Children have the *ability* to say no because the Holy Spirit said He would give them that ability any time they called upon Him for help.

> *Thank you, heavenly Father, for sending the Holy Spirit to help me right* now. *Give me the courage to say "No." Show me what is right to do. Give me the courage to do what You show me to do.*

The number one taunt of children who are trying to pressure another child into sin or misbehavior is this: "Oh, you're just too scared." Teach your child to say, "No, I'm smart. I'm smart enough to know right from wrong. I'm smart enough to know what's good for me and what isn't." Every child needs the assurance that it is OK to say "No," even if he is the only child in the group that does so.

Assure your child that it's not a sin to feel temptation, only to give in to it. Even the Lord Jesus was tempted.

Encourage your child to pray for friends who want to

be like Jesus and who don't want to engage in sinful, harmful activities.

Heavenly Father, please send me friends who love You and who want to do what is right in Your eyes.

42 • Pray for Courage to Take a Stand When the Lord's Name Is Taken in Vain

Be of good courage,
And he shall strengthen your heart,
All you who hope in the Lord.
—Psalm 31:24

Every child I have ever met faces a moment when a friend or acquaintance takes the Lord's name in vain, using it as a byword or a curse word.

Your child will no doubt cringe when that happens. A child who has been taught to respect and love his heavenly Father and the Lord Jesus will want to flee from the presence of someone who doesn't show equal respect and love. What can your child do in these instances?

First, he can pray for courage to take a stand. This is not a time to remain quietly on the sidelines. You may want to teach your child some lines to use, such as "I know that Person you just mentioned. Do you know Him, too?" Or, "I pray to Him. Do you pray to Him, too?" Or, "You just called on His name? What are you wanting Him to do for you?" Encourage your child to pray for boldness:

> *Heavenly Father, help me to be bold right now and to take a stand. Show me exactly what to say to this person. Help me to show love and concern, not hate and ridicule.*

Second, your child can walk away rather than stay in the presence of the offending person. He should not enter into a debate or a fight with him. Often, the person who has taken the Lord's name in vain is embarrassed when challenged. He may turn to vent his anger or ridicule toward your child. Your child does not need to stand and hear that. Walking away takes courage and restraint.

Explain to your child, however, that his encounter with such a person may lead that person to change his life and start following the Lord. The person may not know that his language is offensive to God because he has heard it so often in his environment. Teach your child to pray,

> *Heavenly Father, seal my ears from this abuse and help me not to strike back. Cause my stand for You to bring this person into a new relationship with You so*

they will love You and not use Your name as a curse word.

What should you do when your child tries out curse words that he hears? Punish him just as you would for his breaking any other of the Ten Commandments. Remind your child that the Lord has said, "You shall not take the name of the Lord your God in vain, for the Lord will not hold him guiltless who takes His name in vain" (Ex. 20:7).

Let your child know that you consider cursing to be a serious offense against God and you and your family. Let your child know that the Lord is offended by what your child has said. Encourage your child to pray,

Heavenly Father, I'm sorry about what I have said against You and your Son, Jesus. Please forgive me and help me never to say that again.

Remind your child that it is a high privilege to use the name of the Lord for *good* purposes, a privilege that is never to be abused.

43 • Pray for Comfort in Times of Suffering

Keep me as the apple of Your eye;
Hide me under the shadow of Your wings,
From the wicked who oppress me,
From my deadly enemies who surround me.
                                    —Psalm 17:8–9

In every direction you look today, you will find suffering children. Some are suffering from physical, emotional, or sexual abuse. Others are suffering from addiction, AIDS, leukemia, and other major illnesses. Vast numbers of the world's children are suffering from malnutrition or the effects of war. Although many helps of a practical nature, including counseling and medical assistance, are both appropriate and necessary to lessen the impact of these problems, we can also take comfort in the fact that prayer eases suffering. Teach your child to say no to abuse, to stand up to it, to run away from it, and to always tell you of any abusive behavior they experience or witness.

Heavenly Father, help me to recognize when people are out to do me harm and to have the courage to

*run away from them. If someone I love hurts me
without cause, help me to stand up to them in the
name of Jesus or to tell someone I trust about their
words and actions.*

Assure the child that no abuse or rejection is beyond
the understanding and compassion of Jesus. He paid
the price so that we can be free of any lingering hurts.

*Thank you, Lord Jesus, for taking upon Yourself this
hurt that has come against my life. Praise to You,
Lord Christ, for dying on the Cross so that I can be
free forever of any guilt, harm, or hate that the devil
would try to put on me.*

- Do you know a child who is suffering with a disease?
  Tenderly comfort that child and pray with him,

  *Help me, Lord Jesus. Take away my pain. Take away
  my suffering. Take this disease from my body. Fill me
  with Your healing presence. Give me the strength to
  endure.*

- Do you know a child who is hurting because his
  parents are going through a separation or divorce?
  Assure him that this action is not his fault, nor is it
  God's doing.

  *Help me, Lord Jesus, to feel Your love. Help me not
  to become bitter. Keep hatred out of my heart. Heal*

the hurt that I feel. Help me trust You with my future.

• Do you know a child who has suffered from the news or actual assault of war? Pray with him.

Heavenly Father, please drive the images of war from my mind. Don't let them linger in my memories. Heal me from the fear that I have felt. Help me to put my trust in You. Help me to face the future with hope.

Intercede for your child. Pray daily that your child will be spared the abuse and suffering of this world. Teach your child to pray on a daily basis:

Let me hide away in you, O Lord. Cover me with your protecting feathers the way a hen covers her chicks. Be my shield against harm. Restore my soul.

44 • Pray as You Read the Bible

Teach me Your way, O Lord,
And lead me in a smooth path.
—Psalm 27:11

As you read the Bible with your child—or as your child reads the Bible for herself—encourage your child to include prayer as a part of her devotional time. Teach your child to pray in direct response to the Scriptures.

Before you read a Bible story, or before your child reads the Bible, pray,

> *Help me, heavenly Father, to understand what I am about to read. Give me new insights into Your Word and into Your will for my life. Let me see ways in which I can apply what I am about to read to my daily life.*

Encourage your child to read the Bible aloud to herself. She will get more out of it if she *hears* it read, even if the voice is her own. Children are excited about their own ability to read the Bible.

Teach your child to pray before or after he reads the Word aloud:

> *What I am reading I consider to be a prayer to You, O Lord.*

For example, if your child is reading Psalm 8:1—"O Lord, our Lord,/How excellent is Your name in all the earth,/You who set Your glory above the heavens!"— let your child stop and say,

> *That's my prayer, too, Lord! Your name is excellent. Your glory is higher than the skies. Receive this as my praise to You.*

After you finish a time of Bible reading, pray with your child or teach him to pray,

> *Hide this word away in my mind, heavenly Father. Don't let me forget what I have read. Help me to remember it always. Cause the Holy Spirit to remind me of this passage of Scripture at any time I need to remember it and apply it to my life.*

Many children today are becoming adept at using computers. They understand computer terms and concepts. Encourage your child to memorize passages of Scripture, especially prayers and promises, and then, to pray,

> *Heavenly Father, please file this passage of Scripture on the hard disk of my soul and cause it to come up on the screen of my mind whenever I need it.*

As your child encounters various circumstances and situations in life, encourage him to remind the Lord of

His promises and to recall the Word of the Lord. Teach your child to pray,

> *I ask you boldly to act on that Word of Yours right now, on my behalf. I know that because it is Your Word, I am praying in Your will so I pray as Jesus taught us to pray, Thy will be done on earth—right now—as it is in heaven.*

As your child covers his Bible reading with prayer in this way, the concepts of the Bible and the principles of God are reinforced in his life. The Bible comes more alive to your child, and more applicable. Praying the Scriptures builds your child's faith.

45 • Pray for Courage to Tell the Truth

Teach me good judgment and knowledge,
For I believe Your commandments.
Before I was afflicted I went astray,
But now I keep Your word.
—Psalm 119:66–67

Children lie. Much of their capacity to lie stems from the fact that they have no inborn capacity to differentiate between the concrete world and the world of their imaginations. Fantasy is real to them. Our goal as parents is to confront our children continually— often repeatedly on one subject—with reality and its consequences.

Lying comes in several forms: not telling the whole truth, telling more than the truth (exaggeration), and blatant untruths intended to distort or deceive. All types of lies need to be challenged.

Assure your child that he doesn't need to use lies. Children often tell lies to cover up another sin. Let your child know that there's nothing he has done that is beyond the forgiveness of God. He can speak the truth, repent of his deed, and be forgiven. There's no need to compound a situation with a lie.

Point your child toward prayer when he lies.

Heavenly Father, I'm sorry that I lied. Please forgive me. I know that it was wrong for me to lie. Help me not to lie again.

When you sense your child falling into deception, confront it together in prayer:

Heavenly Father, we want to live in the light of your Truth. Help us to know Your truth. We don't want to be living a lie or to be tricked by deception.

Finally, recognize that lying can easily become a habit. Lying allows a child to manipulate others. Having power over others can be enjoyable for a child, who often feels he has no power over anything. As a result, he lies repeatedly in order to have that temporarily satisfying feeling that comes from having power or "winning" over another person. Confront this attitude in your child any time you encounter it. Don't let your child get away with lying. Encourage your child to pray,

Heavenly Father, help me to develop a desire to tell the truth. Help me to not want to lie. Help me to be able to tell the difference between a lie and the truth.

46 • Pray with Persistence

Then Jesus spoke a parable to them, that men always ought to pray and not lose heart.
—Luke 18:1

Read Luke 18:1–8. The widow in Jesus' parable never gave up. Jesus uses her example as a means of teaching us that we should never give up in our prayers, either. Pray until:

- *You know God's answer.* If you have a question about something, ask God for wisdom. Pray until you receive it. Declare to the Lord,

   I'm not doing anything until You show me what to do. I'm not going to make a decision without knowing that it's the right one in Your eyes.

- *You see the change for good that you want in your life.* Encourage your child to pray for traits that Jesus exhibited in His life. If your child has a tendency to steal, have your child pray daily,

   Help me, heavenly Father, not to steal. Convict me in my heart every time I'm about to take something that isn't mine. Give me the courage not to steal. I don't want to be a thief, Lord. Help me not to be!

By praying daily about a character trait such as this, your child is actually causing his own mind, through prayer, to become more like the mind of Jesus.

- *You either see the miracle you desire, or God takes the desire for something out of your heart.* Pray before you intercede for another person,

    Heavenly Father, I want to pray in Your will. This is my desire. If that isn't Your desire, show me that it isn't.

We insisted that our children be persistent in prayer in two ways.

First, we made certain that our children prayed daily to *"grow in the grace and knowledge of the Lord."*

Second, we insisted that our children pray daily that they might *"be a blessing and not a hindrance"* to the good things that God wanted to do in their lives.

The more times your child prays for or about something, the more important it becomes to him, the more value he places on it, the more vital it is to his life.

47 ● Pray Knowing That Jesus Hears You

And Jesus called a little child to Him, set him in the midst of them, and said, "Assuredly, I say to you, unless you are converted and become as little children, you will by no means enter the kingdom of heaven.

—Matthew 18:2–3

Your child is important to God. Your child has God's ear. In fact, Jesus taught that it is a prerequisite for us *all* to become as little children in our level of faith, trust, adoration, and obedience if we are truly to enter the kingdom of heaven.

Assure your child that Jesus hears his praise. The psalmist challenged us, "Oh, clap your hands, all you peoples! Shout to God with the voice of triumph!" (Ps. 47:1). *All you peoples*—your child certainly is included in that group!

Assure your child that Jesus hears your child's petitions. Your child is as valuable to him as any adult. His needs are important to the Lord.

Assure your child that God hears even his whispers. God isn't hard of hearing. God also pays attention—full, undivided attention—to your child when he prays. Children often live in environments where they are mostly overlooked or their words are ignored.

Assure your child that whenever he calls upon the name of the Lord, he has the Lord's complete and undivided attention. The Lord hears his prayer loud and clear. Furthermore, the Lord understands his prayer, even if he doesn't use adult words. The Lord will not stifle or say "Shhh" to your child's petition.

When you assure your child that the Lord hears, understands, and *desires* his prayers, you are building your child's confidence that God will act on your child's prayers. We are to know a fullness of "joy and peace in believing" (Rom. 15:13). That won't happen for your child unless he first believes that the heavenly Father is hearing him when he prays and that He understands what your child is attempting to say. Give your child that assurance.

Lead your child in thanksgiving,

> *Thank you, heavenly Father, that You hear my prayers! Thank you that You understand me completely and You know what I'm saying. Thank you that You know how to answer my prayer with the very best answer!*

48 • Pray for a Loving and Understanding Heart

When He saw the multitudes, He was moved with compassion for them, because they were weary and scattered, like sheep having no shepherd.
—Matthew 9:36

A spirit of criticism seems to have the Christian world in its grip. Such a spirit robs the *criticizer* far more than the *criticized* because it diminishes in the criticizer a basic sense of "goodness" about the world. It destroys confidence one might place in others and, ultimately, confidence in oneself to live a blameless life above reproach (which is what we are called to do in Christ Jesus).

Encourage your child to look for good in others and to have a loving and understanding heart. Pray with your child,

Heavenly Father, establish in me the ability to see good in other people and to forgive their mistakes. Let me see others as You see them. Give me Your love for them.

Train your child to have compassion. Point out that the positive far outweighs the negative. Encourage your child to edify and build up others. Establish that concept in prayer.

> *Heavenly Father, I pray today for [names]. I ask You to forgive them their sins, make them whole in every area of their beings, and cause them to be filled with Your Holy Spirit so that they will bear the fruit of the Spirit. Help me to see ways in which I can help them to grow in You and to become all that You want them to be.*

In building up others, your child can share his time, prayers, enthusiasm, and ideas. In lifting up others, your child can befriend them, listen to them, and pray with them. Pray with your child,

> *Show me, heavenly Father, a way in which I can be a blessing to my friend. Help me to do what You show me to do.*

Encourage your child to pray for compassion for others, the foremost trait that Jesus exhibited as He ministered to the needs of the people.

- Pray with your child,

> *Help me, heavenly Father, to be courteous to others.*

• Pray with your child,

> *Help me, heavenly Father, not to return evil for evil. Help me not to strike back or try to get even. Help me to plant good seeds even if other people are planting bad ones.*

• Pray with your child,

> *Help me, heavenly Father, not to talk bad about another person. Help me not to spread rumors or to talk back in an angry way to people. Help me to speak kind words even if others speak bad ones.*

Praying for compassion causes a child's empathy for others to grow, and it will keep your child's heart tender and soft toward the Lord and toward others.

49 • Your Prayer Can Be a Song

Be filled with the Spirit, speaking to one another in psalms and hymns and spiritual songs, singing and making melody in your heart to the Lord, giving thanks always for all things to God the Father in the name of our Lord Jesus Christ.

—Ephesians 5:18–20

When our children were teenagers, one year we sang prayers and praise to the Lord in the orchard. We simply made up songs out of our hearts, creating tunes to go with the words we wanted to say to the Lord.

Encourage your child to make up "spiritual songs" that come from the depth of his own being. Make up the words. They don't need to rhyme. Make up the tunes. They don't need to be in perfect rhythm. Let these songs be freewheeling ones that convey meaning and feeling, without regard to perfection of form.

- Sing songs of *praise,* listing the magnificent deeds of God to you, your child, and to others you know.
- Sing songs of *thanksgiving,* citing the many ways in which you are thankful to the Lord for who He is to you and for what He has done on your behalf.
- Sing songs of *worship,* identifying the traits of God and all that He is to you and to your child.

Sing with lifted voice. As you sing, feel free to dance, too! As Psalm 149:2 says, "Let them praise His name with the dance."

You can also encourage your child to sing songs that he already knows—choruses, praise songs, hymns—and to dedicate them to the Lord. Your child can simply say to the Lord,

Heavenly Father, this song is for You.

Give your child the privilege of singing to the Lord as if he was singing to you or to any other person in the room.

Encourage your child to accompany his singing with instruments and clapping. The psalmist did.

Prayer and praise that is framed in song gives your child an opportunity for free-form worship before the Lord. This will acquaint him with the emotion of loving Jesus and of feeling His love envelope and permeate him.

50 • Pray That the Lord Will Give You a Clean Heart

Create in me a clean heart, O God,
And renew a steadfast spirit within me.
—Psalm 51:10

Having a clean heart comes about when your child is forgiven for sin. When your child repents and asks for God's forgiveness, he *is* forgiven. That's the promise of the Lord. Assure your child of that promise.

Obedience is daily. Repentance for acts of disobedience also needs to be daily. Encourage your child to pray:

Heavenly Father, please forgive me for the things that I knew I was supposed to do today and didn't do. Help me to have the courage and the desire to do them tomorrow.

Heavenly Father, please forgive me for the things that I said or did today that made Your heart sad.

Heavenly Father, please forgive me today for disobeying.

Heavenly Father, please forgive me for the thing that I did today that I'm sorry I did.

After your child asks forgiveness of you, make certain that he hears you say that you do, indeed, forgive him. After your child asks forgiveness of the Lord, assure your child that according to God's promises in the Bible, he *is* forgiven by the Lord (1 John 1:9).

Let your child hear you, too, pray for forgiveness. Let Him know that you make mistakes, too. Don't let your child grow up thinking that you, or any other adult, is perfect. A prayer for forgiveness helps assure your child that no sin he commits needs to be "covered up" in order for him to appear perfect before you, others, or the Lord.

A daily prayer for forgiveness:

- Keeps your child free from the burden of guilt.
- Creates a feeling of freedom in your child.
- Causes joy to flood your child's heart.
- Creates an environment for peaceful soul-sleep.
- Eases tension in your home.
- And builds up your child's sense of self-worth and personal value.

Make it a habit to pray daily for forgiveness!

51 • Pray That the Future Will Be Better Than Today

To them God willed to make known what are the riches of the glory of this mystery among the Gentiles: which is Christ in you, the hope of glory.
—Colossians 1:27

Assure your child that the best is yet to come. No matter what the trials, struggles, hardships, or challenges of today, God is there with her now, and He will continue to be there to bring victory out of seeming defeat. Assure your child that you believe with your whole heart that God will make a way for your child, that she will have everything she needs in this life and that she will enjoy eternal life with the Lord in heaven after she dies. What a future!

Talk to your child about what it means to have abundance—spiritually, emotionally, mentally, materially. Point out the generosity of God's blessings to us, the unending flow of good things that He desires for us to have, know, feel, and experience.

• Praise the Lord for your child's future and all the good things that are yet to come.

- Praise the Lord for the family that your child will have one day.
- Praise the Lord for the work that your child will do and for the contribution he will make to his church, community, and nation.
- Praise the Lord for the souls that your child is going to win to the Lord during her life.
- Praise the Lord for the blessing that your child is going to be to others as he prays for them, encourages them, builds them up, loves them, and blesses them in the Name of Jesus.
- Praise the Lord for the spiritual battles that your child is going to win—against the devil and for the advancement of the kingdom of God.
- Praise the Lord for the heavenly home that awaits us, where we will all be able to live together forever and ever with those we love.

Yes, praise the Lord! And even as you praise Him with your child, assure your child that as great as your hopes are for the future, and as good as you envision God's future blessings to be, your hopes and dreams are only a fraction of the hopes and dreams that God has for your child.

II. Teaching Your Child About God

To
Doug Fields
Master Picture Taker

◆ Contents

◆ How to Use These Ideas

This isn't a section of Sunday school lessons about God. It doesn't contain memory verses, Bible quizzes, or homework. There are no lesson plans, summary statements, or materials-needed lists.

Forget all the classroom stuff—these are simple activities that help you open up discussions about God with your child. Each idea helps you create a picture of one aspect of God's character. Here's how to get started:

Step One   *Pick.* Select any idea that interests you. You don't need to go through the book in order (the ideas are arranged alphabetically)—each one is its own picture of God.

Step Two   *Read.* Each idea starts by showing *you* —the parent—how God is like the image described by the title (e.g., "God Is Like an Artist"). Then it suggests an activity to help you convey that picture to your child.

Step Three   *Change.*   Fiddle with the activity so that it fits your child's maturity, skills, and interests. If you don't, some of the ideas may shoot over her head; others will seem childish.* You know your child best—design the activity with her in mind. The discussion questions are just suggestions; feel the freedom to use or discard them as you choose. Also, although most of the ideas are written as one-on-one activities, they can work with two children or as activities for the whole family.

Many of the ideas include an "Other Perspectives" section; here additional activities are described that relate to the picture. You may wish to follow up the main activity with one of these later on. Also, if the

---

* *A note about language:* You may be a father or a mother using these ideas with your son or daughter. So rather than create tiresome sentences like "The parent should keep his or her opinion to him/herself at first so that the child can feel free to express his or her own," I stick with one sex or the other. Some ideas are written with the child as a son, others as a daughter. Either way, the ideas will work with boys or girls.

main idea is impractical for you, maybe an activity in this section will work in its place.

Each idea begins with a Bible verse that suggests the image of God conveyed in the activity. You may wish to use this verse in the discussion. A "Self-Portraits" section concludes many of the ideas. It contains other verses that may help you convey the picture.

These ideas will help your child understand Who he is praying to; that God can be many things and see many things—more things than we could ever find to pray about. The "all mighty" God knows all and is all, so there is no place better to turn when there is a prayer in our hearts—any time, any place.

1 ◆ God Is Like An Artist

Go on an Art Excursion

The heavens declare the glory of God;
the skies proclaim the work of
his hands.   (Psalm 19:1)

Why did God make things so beautiful? He didn't have to. He could have done much worse. He could have made all flowers smell like mildew, all trees gray, all foods taste like cabbage. He might have made all animals identical, every sunset look the same, all seasons equal, the temperature a steady forty degrees year-round.

But God isn't a factory; He's an artist.

When He painted the world, He used a palette containing every color, pattern, shape, texture, odor, taste, and sound. Why so much variety? Maybe He figured He'd have to stare at it for a few years, so He might as well make it interesting. Maybe He figured He was the master artist and we were to be His students, and so He wanted to inspire us.

Or, maybe God uses His art as windows through which we can catch a glimpse of the artist. We can find pictures of His character in His creation.

Art Critics   Visit the library and pick up two books, one containing photos of sculptures or paintings and the other containing photographs of nature.

Look through the first book with your child, stopping periodically to discuss a work of art: "What do you think of this painting [or sculpture]?" "What do you think the artist was trying to tell us?" "What do you think the artist was like? Happy? Sad? Angry? Overwhelmed?" "Why do you think so?" With older children, you can read about one artist and try to see how his art relates to his life. The point is to help your child use the art as a window into the character of its artist. Do this with a few pieces.

Now look at the nature photos. Explain that God, too, is an artist. While looking together at various photos of animals, plants, and landscapes, ask your child the same kinds of questions as before. It's important to encourage her to describe the Artist as revealed in his art—not simply the God she's learned about in Sunday school.

Here are some words you and your child may come up with: *complex, genius, sensitive, delicate, quiet, dangerous, fearless, strong, big, funny.*

Other Perspectives   *Art Hike.* Instead of looking for God's work in books, observe it in a natural setting or at a zoo.

2 ◆ God Is Like a Baby

Conduct a Baby Exam

Today in the town of David a Savior has been born to you; he is Christ the Lord. This will be a sign to you: You will find a baby wrapped in cloths and lying in a manger. (Luke 2:11–12)

God in Diapers Let's face it: Jesus *could* have made a more impressive entrance onto planet Earth. He could have whizzed in on a meteorite. Or skied down a lightning bolt. He could have ridden through the streets on a Bengal tiger or soared in on a giant eagle. (If He had, playing Jesus in the annual Christmas play would certainly be more fun.)

Jesus *could* have arrived in style. Instead, He showed up in a barn.

He was naked and bloody, a crying, drooling, red-faced, puffy-cheeked, helpless newborn baby. They cut His umbilical cord, wrapped Him in cloth, and stuck Him in an animal feed trough. So there you have it: God, Creator of Universe, King of Entire World, makes His grand entrance onto Earth as a thumb-sucking, dirty-diapered infant, born in a barn. (Hence, his habit of forgetting to shut doors.) Jesus didn't just drop out of the sky *disguised* as a human.

He *was* a human, and He arrived here just like everyone else. He even had a belly button to prove it.

Baby Doc   To help your child understand the significance of this God-as-baby concept, conduct a baby exam. A baby brother or sister will do, or you can borrow a friend's infant. You'll need the baby's parent's help with some of the questions. You'll also need some equipment: cloth tape measure (such as a tailor uses), scale, baby toy, a pen. Be sure to wash your hands before beginning the exam. Working together, complete the information form at the end of this section.

When you've completed the exam, serve milk and cookies (or a jar of applesauce) in the baby's nursery and discuss babyhood. Don't look for "right" answers here; just try to get your child to picture Jesus as a real live baby.

Ask: Why do babies cry? Why do they like to be held so much? Why is their skin so soft? With all the crying, dirty diapers, doctor bills, sleepless nights, and snotty noses, why do grown-ups want to have babies? Why does God have us arrive as babies instead of as grown-ups?

Now read together the story of the first Christmas from Luke 2:1–12. Talk about the story: Why did they wrap Jesus in cloths? Why did they put Him in a feed trough (manger)? Did Jesus have a belly button? What kind? Do you think Jesus ever dirtied His diapers? Why did God decide to show up on earth as a baby instead of as a grown-up?

Explain how helpless infants are: When they're cold, they can't put on more clothes or pull up their blanket. When they're hungry, they can't go to the fridge and make a peanut butter sandwich. When they're thirsty, they can't run down to 7-Eleven for a Slurpie. They can't crawl over to get a toy they want, and they can't run out of the house if there's a fire. They can't really do anything for themselves. Without constant attention from other people, they'd die.

You might say something like this to your child: "Have you ever felt helpless? It's a scary feeling, isn't it? One of the reasons God became a helpless baby is that He wanted us to know that *He* knows what helplessness feels like. He knows what diaper rash feels like. He knows what it's like to be cold and not be able to pull up the blanket. He knows how scary it is to be alone in a dark room and hear strange sounds. He knows what it's like to be helpless. So the next time you're feeling helpless or frightened or lonely, talk to Jesus. You can say, 'Jesus, I'm feeling helpless. You know what that feels like, so can You please help me?' He knows exactly how you feel because He was little once too."

Other Perspectives   *Gerber Time.*   Your child can get a better understanding of a baby's helplessness through role-playing. Let your child pretend to be a baby. Feed her a meal. During the meal she is not allowed to talk or point to show you what she wants to eat, nor can she feed herself. Serve her soft and mushy foods only and have her wear a bib (she still possesses one method of expressing distaste). After the meal talk about what she liked and didn't like. Ask her if it was frustrating not to be able to talk. Ask her what a baby does when she's had enough, or is still hungry, or doesn't like the strained carrots?

Baby Flashback.   Together, flip through your child's baby book. Tell her about the trip to the hospital, who came to visit, the list of names you considered, coming home for the first time, how the nursery looked, the child's first crawl, first word, first big laugh.

Baby Exam

Baby's Name _____

Birthdate: _____   Age _____ Months

Number of diaper changes per day: _____

Number of hours of sleep per day: _____

Number of times the baby usually
    wakes up in the night: _____

Weight: _____ pounds _____ ounces

Height: _____ inches

Length of index finger: _____ inches

Length of foot: _____ inches

Circumference of waist: _____ inches

Pulse: _____ beats per minute
    (count for six seconds, multiply by 10)

Grip-the-finger test:

    ☐ strong ☐ medium ☐ light

Eye tracking: Does the baby follow an object moving
across its line of sight ☐ yes ☐ no ☐ kind of

The hair smells like *(check one)*

☐ shampoo   ☐ a hamster cage
☐ soap   ☐ no smell
☐ hair gel   ☐ other:_____

Touch your tongue to the baby's arm: how does
it taste?

(check one)

☐ salty   ☐ like anchovy pizza
☐ oily   ☐ no taste
☐ soapy   ☐ other:_____

Examine the knee: how would you describe it
(check one)

☐ pudgy   ☐ wrinkly and pudgy but in
☐ wrinkly   a cute sort of way
☐ cute   ☐ other_____

Check the belly button:

☐ inny
☐ outy
☐ can't tell yet
☐ no belly button (possibly an alien)

3 ◆ God Is Like a Best Friend

Build a Buddy

I no longer call you servants, because a servant does not know his master's business. Instead, I have called you friends, for everything that I learned from my Father I have made known to you. (Jesus, John 15:15)

Your best friend is one of those few people on the planet who knows all about you, and yet likes you anyway. That's pretty special, considering all the people who've only seen your *good* side and still aren't impressed.

One of the ingredients of best-friendship is letting another person look deep inside you—to see your dreams and fears, to learn your faults and strengths. When Jesus showed up, we humans got to see a side to God He'd never shown to anyone. We met a living, breathing Creator who laughed, cried, played, got mad, went for walks, hung out at parties, and told people what He was thinking. Suddenly, we could all have a new best friend.

Buddy Building Really good friends are hard to find. So why not help your child *build* a best friend? Use pillows and bunched-up towels to form the body, then dress the dummy in clothes. Draw the face on an old pillow case. If you're doing this as a family activity, pair off and build a couple of dummies.

Have your child name his ideal friend and give him a personality. Ask him to describe the buddy's favorite foods, music, sports, hobbies, TV shows, and heroes. To get him talking about the qualities of a best friend, have him describe what makes this friend so special. Ask, "How well does he listen? What's he do when others are putting you down behind your back? What's he do when you tell him a secret? Is there anything about you that you're afraid to tell him? If he found out the absolute worst things about you, would he still be your best friend?"

Now talk about God. "Jesus says He's our friend. But how do we know? Does He match up to our idea of a best friend? Could God ever qualify as your best friend? Does He listen? How do you know? Would He stop being your friend if He knew the worst stuff about you? If God were your best friend, how would He treat you? How would He want to be treated by you?"

It's tough to remain best friends with someone you seldom talk to. Take a moment so each of you can write a short thank-you note to God. The note should start off with "Dear Best Friend God," and then thank Him for things He does that make Him such a good friend. If you want, each of you can read your note.

Other Perspectives   *Start a "Dear Best Friend God" Diary.*   Encourage your child to start a prayer diary made up of thank-you notes and what's-going-on letters written to his best friend, Jesus. He doesn't have to worry about neatness or spelling or even putting a stamp on an envelope—the notes get "faxed" directly to God as he writes them.

Be a Better Friend.   Ask your child to think of two steps he can take this week to be a better friend to someone he knows.

Friendly Proverbs.   The book of Proverbs contains great advice on how to be a friend. Here are some helpful proverbs: 17:17, 18:13, 18:24, 20:19, 22:11, 27:6, 27:9,10.

Self-Portraits

> *Greater love has no one than this, that one lay down his life for his friends.*
> (Jesus, John 15:13)

> *If one falls down, his friend can help him up. But pity the man who falls and has no one to help him up!*   (Ecclesiastes 4:10)

4 ◆ God Is Like A Big Sister or Brother
Talk Big

Whoever does God's will is my brother and sister and mother. (Jesus, Mark 3:35)

Older siblings aren't always loving. Sometimes they can be downright mean. Like when your older brother starts a club with his friends and you want to join, so he makes a rule No Fourth Graders Allowed. You beg him, please can't he make an exception, and he talks it over with his friends and tells you there *is* one way to be in the club, but you have to (a) pour milk in your hair, (b) smear baby powder on your face, and (c) crawl around the block backwards on your hands and knees. So you pour, smear, and crawl, and then shout, "Yipee—I'm in the cluh-ub!" To which your brother and his friends chorus, "I quit!" and run off to start a new club—with no fourth graders allowed.

But this is an extreme case. Older siblings usually aren't *that* bad.

While big brothers and sisters can occasionally exploit their seniority, they really earn their rank when

we're being bullied. My big brother never had to battle any bullies for me. But I knew he was there, three
grades ahead of me and a whole lot stronger and
wiser, ready to stand by my side if I got into trouble.
That assurance made growing up a lot easier.

Jesus is like that. He doesn't fight our battles for
us—life has its share of scraped knees and bloodied
noses. But there's real comfort knowing that He's
there, ready to step in if things turn nasty. Woe to
anyone He catches messing with *His* kid brother or
sister.

Talk Big Talk with your child about what it
means to be a big brother or sister. If your child has
an older sibling, ask: "What's the nicest thing your
big brother has ever done for you? Why did he do it?
How did it make you feel? Has he ever stood up for
you in front of other people? Why?"

If your child *is* a big brother or sister, ask: "Can
you think of the nicest thing you've ever done for
your little brother? Why did you do it? How did that
make you feel? Have you ever stood up for him when
he was being picked on? What made you do it? What
would you do if you saw him being beat up?"

Now talk about his older brother Jesus. Repeat the
child's answers to the question, "What does it mean
to be a big brother?" Ask: "Does Jesus act like an
older brother in any of these ways? How do you think
Jesus feels when He sees you in trouble? Why

doesn't He step in and fight all our battles for us? How can Jesus help you through life's tough times?"

Other Perspectives *Practice Siblinghood.* Talk further about the job of being a sibling. Ask your child to come up with two steps he can take this week to be a better brother or sister.

Be Big. Try to think of a younger child in your neighborhood who doesn't have an older sister or brother. Ask your child to consider acting the part.

5 ◆ God Is Like a Boss

Be the Boss

Well done, good and faithful servant! You have been faithful with a few things; I will put you in charge of many things. Come and share your master's happiness! (Matthew 25:21)

Take a quick walk through your home, and you can probably come up with at least a page of odd jobs that need to be done. But your to-do list looks easy when compared to what needs to be done outside your home: feed the hungry, stop hatred, educate children, clean up the air, heal the sick, and roughly a billion other tasks.

One reason God put us on the planet is to work for Him—to complete our share of this big to-do list. Those who show up to work find out that God is a great boss: He trains us, gives us tasks suited to our gifts and abilities, provides encouragement when we need it, and rewards us when we complete the work.

Big Promotion Kids understand a lot about being a worker, but they don't get many opportunities to be the boss. The next time you have a big household project to do—cleaning the garage, washing the windows, preparing for overnight guests—switch jobs with your child. Make her the boss and you the worker. Sit down together and make a list of all the specific tasks, then let her tell you who is supposed to do what. Then get to work!

Be sure to ask lots of questions and ask for her help throughout the job. Treat her like a real boss, and respect her authority. If you've modeled good management in the past, she'll encourage you, give you coffee breaks, and lend a hand. If you've been more of a dictator than a good boss, that's what you'll get from her.

When the work is done, talk about how she felt being the boss and how you felt being the worker.

Explain that God is our boss, and we are His workers. What jobs does He have for us? How do you find out what He wants done? How does He help us do them? Does He pay us? How? What do you think is God's definition of a good worker?

Wrap things up by asking her to think of one job God wants her to accomplish this week. What is it? When will she work on it? Will He pay her for it? How?

Other Perspectives *Junior Management.* Your child may be in a leadership position on a sports team or when looking after younger brothers and sisters. Have her describe her responsibilities, and ask her to think of one or two steps she can take to become a better leader.

6 ◆ God Is Like Bread

Hold a Bake Session

I am the bread of life.   (Jesus, John 6:48)

I still remember my favorite after-school TV snack. It wasn't Hostess Twinkies, or Vanilla Wafers, or Goldfish crackers. It was Wonder Bread. I'd take a slice, peel off the crust and roll the rest into a white doughy ball. Then I'd pop the ball into my mouth and try to suck on it, without chewing, until the next TV commercial. If the show was really suspenseful (Gilligan spotting a ship, for instance), I'd devour a half-dozen slices before the closing credits. I could have eaten an entire loaf that way, but I never got a chance: my brothers and sisters enjoyed the same snack, so we'd run out of bread before we ran out of hunger.

I somehow got over my craving for Wonder Bread, but other cravings have taken its place. Now I hunger for new cars, electronic gadgets, tropical vacations, the constant approval of others. And I still run out of "bread" before I run out of hunger.

Deep inside we're all hungry. Yet nothing on earth seems to satisfy the hunger—not for long anyway. Just as God gave us physical hunger to remind us we must eat to survive, He gives us a spiritual hunger to tell us we need Him to truly live.

Hold a Bake Session Spend an afternoon baking in the kitchen. If you have enough equipment, make several loaves of bread and give some away to friends. While the bread is baking, sit down with your child and talk about hunger: How do we know when we are hungry? Why do our bodies work this way? What happens if we don't eat when we are hungry?

Talk about other things people crave. For instance, when someone is acting obnoxiously, we say he's "starved for attention." Can your child think of other things people crave (love, alcohol, drugs, gambling, money, new clothes, cars)? We get hungry for all sorts of things, but it seems we can never get enough to satisfy our cravings. Wouldn't it be nice if there was something so good and filling that it satisfied our cravings and took away the hunger?

Now read what Jesus says in John 6:35: "I am the bread of life. He who comes to me will never go hungry, and he who believes in me will never be thirsty." Talk about what this verse means. How does God take away our hunger?

Other Perspectives *Help the Hungry.* It's tough to meet peoples' spiritual needs when they have great physical needs. Have your family sponsor a needy child through a development organization such as Compassion International or World Vision. The letters and monthly support you send to your child provide both kinds of nourishment.

Break Bread. Instead of saying grace before a family meal, take a loaf of bread, break off pieces for everyone, and explain that this bread reminds us of another kind of Bread that keeps us alive: Jesus.

Self-Portraits

> *When your words came, I ate them;*
>   *they were my joy and my heart's delight,*
> *for I bear your name,*
>   *O LORD God Almighty.*   (Jeremiah 15:16)

> *And Jesus took bread, gave thanks and broke it, and gave it to them, saying, "This is my body given for you; do this in remembrance of me."*   (Luke 22:19)

7 ◆ God Is Like a Carpenter
Work with Wood

Unless the LORD builds the house, its builders labor in vain. (Psalm 127:1)

A carpenter doesn't start a project by swinging a hammer. In fact, that's just about the last thing he does. First he builds the piece in his mind; he decides what it will look like, what materials and tools he'll need. If the design is complicated, he'll then use pencil and paper to sketch out the design and write up a list of materials. Then he gathers the tools and materials together. Finally, he's ready to start swinging the hammer.

God does the same thing with our lives. First He designs us. Next, He gathers up the tools and materials He'll need to make it happen. Then He gets to work.

By the time He shows His project to anyone else (generally on our birthdays), He's already gotten pretty far with the construction. But there's plenty more work to do—walking, talking, learning, growing. To do the job right He uses priceless tools with names like *parent, teacher,* and *friend.*

He starts on the project before you're born, and

He works on it throughout your entire life. He's a perfectionist, and so it takes Him exactly that long to do you right.

Wood Work Build something together with your child—a book stand, birdhouse, doghouse, anything you can make with a minimum of tools. You can get ideas for simple wood projects from a library book. Design the project together. Make a list of tools and materials, and go together to the hardware store.

When you're finished with the project, talk about it: Did the finished piece come out as you expected? What was the toughest part of the job? If you built another one, what would you change?

Now talk about God the Carpenter. Ask your child: "What tools does God use to shape and build you? When God started building you, did He work from a plan? Is He finished with you? If you could look on His design for you, what do you think He wants you to be like in two years? What do you think is the toughest part of the job for Him?"

God has made each of us unique, and He's still working on us. Discuss what God might be doing in your child's life right now. Ask, "Is there anything you can do right now to make God's work easier?"

Other Perspectives *Jesus the Carpenter.*
Watch a carpenter at work. Perhaps his hands are
tough and calloused; his arms may be muscular and
tan. Contrast this image of Jesus as carpenter with the
pictures seen in Sunday school. Ask, "Did Jesus ever
hit His thumb with a hammer? Did He sweat? Get
tired? Feel proud of something He made?"

Self-Portraits

> *You created my inmost being;*
>   *you knit me together in my mother's womb.*
> *I praise you because I am fearfully and*
> *wonderfully made;*
>   *your works are wonderful,*
>   *I know that full well.*
> *My frame was not hidden from you*
>   *when I was made in the secret place.*
> *When I was woven together in the depths of the*
> *earth,*
>   *your eyes saw my unformed body.*
> *All the days ordained for me were written in*
> *your book*
>   *before one of them came to be.*
> (Psalm 139:13–16)

> *Being confident of this, that he who began a*
> *good work in you will carry it on to*
> *completion until the day of Christ*
> *Jesus.*   (Philippians 1:6)

8 ◆ God Is Like a Child

Spy on Preschoolers

Therefore, whoever humbles himself like this child is the greatest in the kingdom of heaven. (Jesus, Matthew 18:4)

Once upon a time, childhood was when kids could be harmlessly ignorant of adult privileges and vices such as sex, drugs, violence, materialism, and vanity. Not anymore. These "adult" issues and problems are now epidemic among teenagers. And many of the same preoccupations are showing up in elementary schools. Today's kids are growing up way before their time.

When children grow up too fast, they leave behind more than hand-me-downs: they discard a closet filled with beautiful qualities that God intended for them to keep all their lives. Gifts like innocence, lack of prejudice, forgiveness, humor, the ability to play and dream. The tragedy is that these are some of the qualities that make us most like God. Maybe when we start to realize how childlike God is, we'll stop trying to grow up so fast.

Kid Observation Ask your child to go with you
on a scientific journey to study the habits of a strange
and fascinating creature. Go to a nearby nursery
school (with permission) or a playground and point
out the creatures you have come to observe:
preschoolers. Sit near the play equipment so you can
watch the subjects up close. Mention that some people believe preschoolers have vivid imaginations, are
quick to forgive and forget, and are highly skilled at
making friends. Your purpose is to look for those
kinds of behaviors.

As the two of you point out some of these behaviors, talk about why they're common among small
children. For example: Why is it so easy for
preschoolers to be angry with someone one minute
and best friends with them the next? Why is it
tougher for older people to do the same? Why are
preschoolers so social? Why don't they seem to care
how they look? Why don't adults play and dream as
little kids do?

As you observe these and other qualities of childhood, explain that God must be a lot like a child
because He has many childlike qualities. Ask her if
she can think of stories from the Bible that demonstrate those traits.

Take a moment to express the godly qualities you
see in your child. Be sure to give specific examples of
times when she demonstrated those qualities so she
knows exactly what you mean. When you give her a

mental picture of herself exhibiting those traits, she's less likely to grow out of them as she leaves childhood behind.

Other Perspectives *Photo Flashback.* You can take your child back to her early childhood with photo albums, scrapbooks, and home videos. As the two of you review her past, tell her stories of times when she acted like God the Child.

Jesus the Kid. We don't know a lot about Jesus as a child, but the Bible gives us a few ideas. Read Luke 2:40–52 together and ask your child to describe what she thinks Jesus was like as a kid.

Self-Portraits

> *And [Jesus] said: "I tell you the truth, unless you change and become like little children, you will never enter the kingdom of heaven."* (Jesus, Matthew 18:3)

> *"And whoever welcomes a little child like this in my name welcomes me. But if anyone causes one of these little ones who believe in me to sin, it would be better for him to have a large millstone hung around his neck and to be drowned in the depths of the sea."* (Jesus, Matthew 18:5, 6)

9 ◆ God Is Like a Comedian

Host a Comedy Show

Our mouths were filled with laughter, our tongues with songs of joy.   (Psalm 126:2)

We don't learn much about God's sense of humor at church; we have to pick it up through our own observations. Imagine for a moment these natural phenomena, and see if you don't come to the same conclusion: monkeys in trees, prairie dogs sunbathing, a duck landing on a lake, a dog chasing its tail, a sea otter doing *anything*.

If the clowns of the animal kingdom don't convince you, observe children doing what comes naturally, like yawning loudly at a boring speech. Or burping in church. Or a baby oozing strained beets out of its mouth—definitely not a learned behavior. Small children know when to laugh, even before we've had a chance to teach them what "funny" means.

Our world is filled with all sorts of funny stuff that humans had nothing to do with. So if we didn't create all this comedy, who did?

Comedy Show Help your kids put together a comedy show starring themselves. They can do skits, tell jokes, even show a funny video they made up. They can invite their friends to be part of the show or to be the audience.

After all the funny business, have a talk about laughter. Tell of a time you got the giggles when you were supposed to be serious. Ask: "Why do we sometimes laugh the hardest when we shouldn't be laughing at all? Why did God give us laughter? Where do we get a sense of humor? Do you think God likes to watch us laugh? Does God ever laugh?"

Other Perspectives *Good Fun, Bad Fun.* Sometimes we laugh at another person's expense. Talk about the difference between the fun that builds people up and that which tears them down. Ask your child to come up with examples of each.

Family Jokes. Pull off fun surprises and jokes for your kids. Throw a birthday party when it is *not* his birthday. Instigate a shaving cream fight while you're washing the car together. Bury a treasure in the yard, and give your child a pirate's map to find it.

10 ◆ God Is Like a Counselor

Hold a Counseling Session

All this also comes from the LORD Almighty, wonderful in counsel and magnificent in wisdom.   (Isaiah 28:29)

Many people call themselves counselors: marriage and family counselors, legal counselors, spiritual counselors, camp counselors, career counselors, guidance counselors. While these professions represent a wide variety of disciplines, counselors of any type have share a few things in common. A good counselor in any profession is wise, respected, and knows how to listen and reason.

When the prophet Isaiah predicted Jesus's coming, he said that people would call him Wonderful Counselor. For good reason: Jesus is wiser than anyone on the planet, His excursion down here earned our respect, and He's a whiz at listening to and reasoning with us. Wonderful Counselor.

This is a crazy, complicated world. Without wise counsel, there's no way to see through the confusion and make the right choices. Counselor God is ready to listen, eager to help.

Counseling Session   Have your child pretend he's your counselor. Tell him you need his advice about an actual conflict you're having with a friend or coworker. Explain the situation, being sure to describe your *feelings*. For instance, he may not know what it's like to be passed up for a promotion, but he knows what rejection feels like.

When you explain the situation, ask him specific questions about what he thinks you should do. Listen carefully to his answers, and respond with more questions if he's being vague or doesn't seem to understand. The point is to get him to realize the critical responsibility a counselor has. You're counting on him to be a listening ear, to help you see the problem more clearly, and to give you wise advice about what to do.

When the counseling session is over, thank him for his help. Then talk about the job of counselor. Ask: "Have you ever gone to a friend for advice, but, instead of listening, he started telling you what to do before he even heard what your problem was? Have you ever thought of the solution to a problem while explaining the problem to someone else? What makes a good counselor?"

Now talk about Counselor God: "Does God fit the description of a good counselor? Why don't people go to Him with their decisions and problems more often? When you've explained a problem to God, how do you know what advice He's giving you? Is there anything you'd like to talk over with Him now?"

By the way, be sure to follow through on your counseling session by telling your child what you ended up doing about the conflict you discussed. Thank him for helping you clarify your thinking. And if you took his advice, let him know it.

Other Perspectives   *Repeat the Session.*   It's not a bad idea to go to your kids for counsel occasionally. Knowing that you trust and value their opinion is important to them. And you may be surprised at how well they can simplify a confusing problem.

Polish the Mirror.   Kids learn their listening and questioning skills from parents. So if your child is having a tough time with these skills, perhaps you need to work on your own. Each day, sit down for a few minutes with your child. Listen carefully and question thoughtfully.

Self-Portraits

> *To God belong wisdom and power;*
> *counsel and understanding are*
> *his.*   (Job 12:13)

11 ◆ God Is Like a Dad

Conduct a Dad Survey

How great is the love the Father has lavished on us, that we should be called children of God! And that is what we are!   (1 John 3:1)

A little boy's dad took him to a department store packed with hurried and noisy shoppers. Halfway down a crowded aisle, the boy got scared and reached out to take a firm grip of his dad's pant leg. But when he looked up, the man in the pants wasn't his dad. It was a stranger, who pulled his leg away from the boy and walked away. The boy panicked.

Desperately reaching out with the other hand, he found another pant leg and grasped it with all his strength. But instead of pulling the cloth from his grip, this man reached down to pat the boy's head. The big hand, the smell of the aftershave left no doubt: this was his dad. He had been walking beside him the whole time—the boy just didn't know where to look.

God the Dad walks beside us all the time. As His

sons and daughters, we can reach out and grab His leg. He won't pull away.

Dad Survey To most kids, dads are dads. They've never really taken the time to analyze the job of being a father. The Dad Survey gives kids a chance to see what constitutes a good dad. Run off several copies of the survey at the end of this section. Have your child call or visit four dads she respects. Ask her to interview these dads by asking them the questions on the survey.

When she's done with all four, talk about the results. Ask: "After hearing what these dads said, what do *you* think are a dad's three most important responsibilities? Why? What did the dads enjoy most about being dads? What were their least favorite parts of being dads?"

Your child can probably think of dads who aren't good dads—maybe even some who beat up on their kids or yell at them too much. She may know kids who don't have dads for one reason or another. Tell her that God knows that some kids have dads they can't hug, or climb on, or cry to. So God has decided to be their dad. In fact, God is everyone's dad, and we're His sons and daughters.

- Like any dad, God doesn't like it when we do bad or selfish things.

- But like a great dad, God doesn't stop loving us when we do.
- Like any dad, God is hurt when we ignore Him or choose to disobey.
- But like a great dad, God never ignores us.

God is a great dad, and He loves His children more than anything else in the whole world.

Other Perspectives   *Poster Dad.*   A survey may be too difficult for younger children. Instead, give the child a sheet of poster paper and crayons or markers. Have him draw pictures of his dad doing his favorite and least favorite things. Afterward, discuss the pictures and the dad they represent.

Dear Dad Letter.   One way to make praying easier is to have the child write a thank-you note to God the Dad. The letter can start off with Dear Dad; the rest is up to her.

Parable of the Forgiving Dad.   The hero of the story in Luke 15:11–31 is not the prodigal son, but the dad. Read the parable together, and compare that dad to God the Dad.

Dad Survey

What are the 3
most important responsibilities of a dad?

1. _____

2. _____

3. _____

What's your favorite part of being a dad?

_____

_____

_____

What's your *least* favorite thing about being a dad?

_____

_____

_____

12 ◆ God Is Like a Doctor

Visit the Doctor's Office

He heals the brokenhearted and binds up their wounds.   (Psalm 147:3)

Doctors can get us to do just about anything.

"Take off your clothes and put on this ridiculous gown."

"Sure."

"Now open your mouth while I jam a Popsicle stick into your throat."

"AHHH."

"I need a sample—fill this cup."

"Where's the bathroom?"

If anyone else told you to do those things, you'd either punch him in the nose or run for your life. So why do we tolerate pain and embarrassment from doctors? Because we trust that they know what's best for us. We believe they have our best interest at heart, and whatever stupid or painful things they make us go through are necessary to make us better and keep us healthy. It's called faith.

Doctor Jesus works the same way. Sometimes He asks us to do things that are painful or embarrassing. We can't figure out why, but we trust that He knows what He's doing, and doing it to make us better.

The Doctor's Office   If your child has a visit with the doctor scheduled soon, turn the appointment into an opportunity to learn about God. On the way to the doctor's office, talk about why you're going. Ask, "Why don't we try to be our own doctor? Why is a trained doctor better? What might happen if you never went to the doctor?"

While you're with the doctor, encourage your child to ask her a few questions, such as: "Why did you choose to be a doctor? What do you like about it? What don't you like? Do you ever have patients who don't do what you tell them? Why don't they do what you say? What happens to them?"

On the way home, talk about the appointment. Ask, "Did the doctor do anything that made you uncomfortable or embarrassed? Did she do anything painful? Why did you do as you were told? Can you think of ways that God is like a doctor? Does He ever ask you to do things that are embarrassing or painful? Does He always take away your pain? Can you think of an example when physical pain could be a good thing? How about emotional pain—rejection, heartbreak, failure—why does God let us suffer?"

Wrap up the conversation by asking your child if

she can think of anything Doctor God is asking her to do to make her healthier. "Is there some lesson He's teaching right now? Are you going through any kind of trial or emotional pain that God can use to strengthen you? How can that experience make you better? What can you do right now to learn from the pain?"

Other Perspectives *Meet Someone Who's Been Healed.* Talk together with someone who's come through a major emotional or physical trauma such as an addiction, divorce, severe injury, or a long-term illness. Ask the person what part God plays in the healing process. Did he doubt God's love, intentions, or existence? In what ways is life better now?

Trial Advice. Read James 1:2–12 together and try to figure out what James was saying about the benefits of trials. Is it really possible to consider them good? What's the reward for withstanding them?

Self-Portraits

> *O LORD my God, I called to you for help and you healed me.* (Psalm 30:2)

13 ◆ God Is Like a Dreamer
Daydream Together

Delight yourself in the LORD and he will
give you the desires of your heart.
Commit your way to the LORD; trust in
him and he will do this.
(Psalm 37:4, 5)

Some of humankind's biggest accomplishments started out as dreams. What if there was a "back road" to China? Hello America. What if man could fly? Try an airplane. What if there was a vaccine for polio? Dr. Salk pursued the dream.

Dreaming is a beautiful gift given to us by a God who dreamed the universe into existence. It's a priceless gift in an imperfect world. In a perfect world, *what is* is the best it can be. There's no need to ask *what if?* when it's impossible to imagine something better.

But our world is far from perfect. You *can* imagine a better world and even entertain the thought of trying to get there. You can dream. You can ask *what if?*

Sometimes God the Dreamer plants His dream in the hearts of His people. The Israelites dreamed of the "promised land," so wonderful it flowed with milk and honey. They dreamed of a temple of God in Jerusalem. They dreamed of a Messiah. God fulfilled those dreams through His people.

The good news is God still dreams, and He plants His dreams in our hearts. Our job is to take a look inside to discover the dreams He's given us to fulfill.

Brainstorm   Little kids dream and imagine constantly. But somewhere along the way to adulthood they cut down on asking *what if?* and get preoccupied with *what is*. You can help them hold onto this precious gift by dreaming with them. Here are a few brainstorm sessions you and your child can try:

- What if you decided to build a new house for your family? Money is no object. What does it look like? Does it have an indoor pool? Are there water slides from every bedroom? How about a rope swing from your room to the kitchen—in case you're hungry for a banana in the middle of the night? Does the garage convert to a drive-in theater? You get the idea. Sketch your dream house on paper, interview family members about what they'd like.
- What if the school board asked you to design a new school, hire new teachers, change the classroom size, come up with new subjects? What does the new school look like? How many students are in each class? What are the teachers like? What happens when the teacher sends kids

to the office? What subjects are taught at the school?

• What if you decided to build an amusement park in your neighborhood? What are the rides like? Describe one of the roller coasters.

• What if you were elected President? What things would you change?

• What if you decided to cure a disease? Which one would you work on? How would you figure out the cure? What effect would your accomplishment have on others?

After your brainstorm session, talk about God the Dreamer. Did God do a similar thing when He decided to create the world? Does God still dream? What are some of His dreams now? Are they idle dreams, or does He work on making them come true? How does God make His dreams come true?

Mention some examples of people who dreamed for God and had their dreams come true: Joshua and Jericho, David with Goliath (Fight Goliath?!—dream on, David!), Daniel in Babylon, Nehemiah rebuilding Jerusalem. "How do you dream for God? Do you have dreams right now that might be part of God's dreams too? How can God help you make them come true?"

14 ◆ God Is Like an Eagle
Study Eagles

. . . he guarded him as the apple of his eye, like an eagle that stirs up its nest and hovers over its young, that spreads its wings to catch them and carries them on its pinions. (Deuteronomy 32:10, 11)

The great moment in an eagle's life is when it learns to fly. There are no classroom lessons, textbooks, films, lectures, or homework. The mother just transports the eaglet on her wings to a high altitude and lets it fall—a crash course, as it were.

Well, not quite. She swoops down and catches the child before the course is over. Then she repeats the lesson until the eaglet gets the hang of it. With each test flight the child's wings grow stronger. It learns balance and flight control, and how to soar inside columns of rising air. Eventually it learns to take off, fly, and land on its own. Another eagle earns its wings.

God the Eagle does the same thing to us. Sometimes He drops us into unfamiliar and frightening situations. We learn to fly by faith, faith that He knows what He's doing; that He loves us so much He won't allow us to be destroyed; that flying will be so incredible that it's worth all He's putting us through to learn.

Eagle Study   Read a book together about eagles. Talk about how they take care of their young, learn to fly, how they soar. Ask your child to imagine what it would be like to learn to fly that way. "What would you be thinking as your mother let you go? Would you think she was trying to kill you? Why does she teach flying this way? Does *she* ever get scared for her child?"

Now talk about God the Eagle. Sometimes God introduces us to new ways of thinking or acting by putting us in new situations where we learn out of necessity. Ask your child to think of examples? Has he ever been scared that God wouldn't catch him?

Self-Portraits

> *You yourselves have seen what I did to Egypt,*
> *and how I carried you on eagles' wings and*
> *brought you to myself.*   (Exodus 19:4)

> *But those who hope in the* Lord
> *will renew their strength.*
> *They will soar on wings like eagles;*
> *they will run and not grow weary,*
> *they will walk and not be faint.*
> (Isaiah 40:31)

15 ◆ God Is Like a Fire
Burn Something

. . . for our God is a consuming fire.   (Hebrews 12:29)

As a child I learned a lot about life by sitting next to a fire at summer camp. My friends and I would argue and criticize and joke the entire day, but as soon as we sat around the campfire, our conversation changed. What we said around the fire was deep— deeply funny, deeply serious, deeply moving, and now rooted deep in my memory. It was as if the fire reached inside us and drew out thoughts and feelings we didn't even know we had.

God was a frequent topic around those fires. Maybe the mystery of fire made us contemplate the mystery of God. Or maybe it was the warmth of the fire that spurred our conversations. Ten feet away from the fire, the air was as cold as if there was no fire. Three feet away and you were comfortable and warm. Move one foot closer and it singed the hair on your arms.

God is like a fire. He brings warmth and lights up the darkest places in our lives. He thaws out our hearts until we begin to feel things inside we didn't know were there. If we move too far away from God, we feel cold and alone. Get close, and we are glad to be counted among His friends instead of His enemies.

Build a Fire   You don't have to go to summer camp to have a campfire. Find a park or beach where campfires are allowed. Bring firewood, kindling, paper, matches, and some marshmallows.

After roasting marshmallows, ask your child, "Why do people enjoy sitting around a fire? What would life be like without fire? What's your favorite thing about a fire? What happens if you get too careless with a fire? What happens when you get too far away?"

Now steer the conversation toward God. Explain that the Bible says God is like a fire. Ask, "Do you think that's true? In what ways? If God is like a fire, how can we be sure to stay warm? Does God ever burn people? How? What can you do to keep from getting burned? What happens when you move too far away from God? How can you prevent that from happening?"

Other Perspectives   *Homemade Fire.* If building an outdoor fire isn't possible, you can use a fireplace. Make the activity special by allowing your child to stay up past bedtime to enjoy the fire with you.

16 ◆ God Is Like a Fort

Take a Fort Tour

The Lord is a refuge for the oppressed,
a stronghold in times of
trouble.   (Psalm 9:9)

Every kid builds forts, though not every kid calls it a fort. Sometimes the "fort" is called a spaceship, pirate ship, treehouse, hideout, or playhouse.

My nephew Brice builds couch forts—sofa cushions and blankets carefully arranged to form a fortress in the living room. He also makes forts from cardboard boxes, trash cans, and anything else he can find on the side of the house. He builds his forts to protect himself from all sorts of hazards, including naptime and an over-exuberant dog that tries to lick his face off. Soon he'll graduate to a fort made from wood and carpet scraps, stuck in a tree or gully near his house. I'm sure it will have a skull-and-cross-bones drawn on the door.

When he grows out of that one, he'll convert his room into a fort. It will be plush as fortresses go, complete with stereo, maybe a phone, and wall-to-wall piles of games, sports equipment, and clothes. The sign on the door will say "Trespassers will be eaten!" After that, he'll get a *moving* fort—a car. This time the sign will be on the license plate frame —"If you don't like the way I drive, stay off the sidewalk."

Why all these forts? Why do we have this need to establish hiding places we can call our own? Instinctively we seem to know that the world can be a dangerous place. I think we build strongholds where we can feel safe from the scary things in life.

God is like a fort. We can run to Him when we're overwhelmed by the world's troubles and fears. We can escape to the fort of God's presence.

Fort Tour   Ask your child for a tour of his secret hiding place. If he doesn't have one at the moment, build a fort together. Sit together in the fort and talk about what makes forts so special. Ask, "Why do kids like to build forts? What do you think about when you're sitting in yours?"

Talk about how people throughout history used fortresses to protect themselves from attacking enemies. When an enemy army swept into a village, the people would run for the fortress to save their lives. The gates would be locked, the doors closed, and the people would be safe from their enemies.

Now explain how God is like a fort. When you're scared and being chased by enemies, you can take your heart to him and he keeps it safe. Close the discussion by assuring your child that God promises to be the fort for his heart. When he's in pain or frightened by anything, he can run to God, call out for help, and God will open up the fortress gates and hide his heart inside.

Other Perspectives   *Room Forts.*   For lots of kids, especially older ones, their bedroom is their refuge. Ask if you can take a tour. Have your child explain what is on the walls and shelves, and why. Ask what he likes most and least about his room.

Self-Portraits

> *You are my hiding place;*
>   *you will protect me from trouble*
>   *and surround me with songs of*
> *deliverance.*   (Psalm 32:7)

> *But I will sing of your strength,*
>   *in the morning I will sing of your love;*
> *for you are my fortress,*
>   *my refuge in times of trouble.*
> (Psalm 59:16)

> *I will say of the LORD, "He is my refuge and*
> *my fortress,*
> *my God, in whom I trust."*   (Psalm 91:2)

17 ◆ God Is Like a Foundation
Build a Wall

See, I lay a stone in Zion, a tested stone, a precious cornerstone for a sure foundation; the one who trusts will never be dismayed. (Isaiah 28:16)

With most things in life, if you get off to a rough start you can go back and fix the problem later. If you don't like the introduction to a story you're writing, you can finish the story and then go back and re-write the opening. If you get a bad grade on the first test in a class, you can still pull off a high grade by doing well on other tests.

But when it comes to building a stone wall, if you don't set that first stone straight, everything above it will always be crooked or unstable no matter how you try to compensate. Tearing down the wall and starting over is the only option.

God wants us to build our lives on a firm and straight foundation.

Build a Wall Build a wall with your child using blocks, bricks, boxes, books—anything you can stack. Start the activity by building the wall on something unstable—crooked ground, crumpled up newspapers, lumpy pillows. The wall is okay for the first course or two, but then it becomes obvious that the structure is crooked and getting worse the higher you go.

Knock down this wall and start over. This time build upon flat, solid ground. Compare the stability of the two walls. Now talk with your child about the importance of a solid foundation. Explain that the world is a big and wild place, with lots of people offering answers to anyone who will listen. God says we need to believe something solid and true, or we'll fall apart when tough times come. Talk about the foundation God has in mind for our lives.

Self-Portraits

> *God's household [is] built on the foundation of the apostles and prophets, with Christ Jesus himself as the chief cornerstone.*   (Ephesians 2:20)

> *For in Scripture it says: "See, I lay a stone in Zion,*
> *a chosen and precious cornerstone,*
> *and the one who trusts in him*
> *will never be put to shame."*
> (1 Peter 2:6)

18 ◆ God Is Like a Genius
Take a Trivia Quiz

Among all the wise men of the nations and in all their kingdoms, there is no one like you. (Jeremiah 10:7)

God knows everything, including answers to age-old questions such as . . .

- How many angels *can* dance on the head of a pin?
- Can God make a rock so heavy he can't lift it?
- How high is up?

And he knows a few other things, like the number of hairs on your head. The names and addresses of everyone you've ever cut in front of on the freeway. He knows the number of calories in a Hershey's Kiss the size of Kilimanjaro. He knows the birthdates of all your family's pets clear back through the ages starting with the day your distant Uncle Ug discovered a litter of saber-toothed tigers in the back of his cave.

God knows all your problems, including the ones you won't admit to (and a dozen more you don't even know you have). God the Genius knows about your biggest dreams, your worst fears. He's the only one who knows that you still check under your bed for the bogeyman. He knows the best answer to your toughest dilemmas.

What's more amazing than how much God knows? How little we ask Him for the answers. Look at it this way. Here's someone who knows *everything,* and most of us don't bother to ask Him for advice. Yet he's been known to share His knowledge with those who really desire it.

M&M's Candy Quiz Play a game with your child using questions from a trivia book or the cards from a trivia game. Set a bowl of M&M's candy on the table. For every simple question answered correctly, take one candy; tougher questions are worth two candies, and the toughest questions pay three. Alternate asking and being asked; play until the candies are gone.

After the game, talk about how smart God is. There isn't a question in the world that God can't answer. Ask, "What are some things that would be impossible for humans to know (number of grains of sand on the beach, number of stars in the sky, why God allows good people to die, what heaven is like)? If God is a genius, why doesn't He share all His knowledge with us? Does He share *any* of it? How?"

19 ◆ God Is Like a Gift
Open a Present

For it is by grace you have been saved, through faith—and this not from yourselves, it is the gift of God. (Ephesians 2:8)

You can't earn God—He's a gift. Wouldn't He *have* to be? Can you imagine earning Him by, let's say, selling magazine subscriptions through the school's fund-raising drive? You have to sell ten subscriptions to earn a nifty pen-and-pencil set and 50 to get a Walkman. At that rate, how many would it take earn the Creator of the universe?

You can't redeem your frequent flyer miles for Him, nor can you win Him with a lottery ticket. You can't buy, lease, rent, earn, or win Him. He's a gift: you take it, open it, and say thank you.

Open a Present Buy and wrap a gift your child would enjoy. Put a tag on it with his name, but don't write who it's from.

Walk in the room with the gift and announce that you found it at the door. Here's how the ensuing conversation might go:

MOM   Hey, look what I found at the front door.

SON   Who's it for?

MOM   The tag says it's for you.

SON   Great! Let me have it.

MOM   Hold on. Maybe it's a birthday gift you shouldn't open until then.

SON   My birthday isn't for three more months!

MOM   You can wait that long.

SON   No way!

MOM   Well, maybe it's a Christmas present.

SON   Right! I can't wait all year! Please let me have it.

MOM   Well, I'm not even sure it's for you. Maybe it's for someone else with the same name. Wouldn't it be horrible if you opened someone else's gift by mistake.

SON   Mom! Let me open it!

MOM   (shaking it) Hmm . . . I wonder what it is?

SON   Mom!

MOM   I'll give it to you in a minute, but first let me tell you something. I'm the one who got you this gift. I didn't get it for any reason except that you're my son and I love you. You didn't earn it. I'm not giving it to you as a reward for good grades, or because you cleaned your room, or because you were nice to your little sister. Believe it or not, if you hadn't done those things, I still would give you this gift.

Give the child the gift, and let him open it. Afterwards, explain to him that God has given us Himself as a gift. Some people try to earn God's love. They figure that if they do enough nice things, or go to church every week, or give money to charity, God will decide to love them. But God is priceless. No one can afford to buy Him. God's love is a gift. There's nothing you can do but take it, open it, and thank Him for it.

Self-Portraits

> *For the wages of sin is death, but the gift of God is eternal life in Christ Jesus our Lord.* (Romans 6:23)

> *Thanks be to God for his indescribable gift!* (2 Corinthians 9:15)

> *Every good and perfect gift is from above, coming down from the Father of the heavenly lights, who does not change like shifting shadows.* (James 1:17)

> *Each one should use whatever gift he has received to serve others, faithfully administering God's grace in its various forms.* (1 Peter 4:10)

20 ♦ God Is Like a Guide

Take a Trust Walk

I will lead the blind by ways they have not known, along unfamiliar paths I will guide them; I will turn the darkness into light before them and make the rough places smooth. (Isaiah 42:16)

Life is a jungle. It's full of beautiful sights, exciting adventures, and wonderfully friendly natives. But it's also dangerous—wild animals, deadly situations, and a few *un*friendly natives. If you want to experience the best that life has to offer, you need someone who knows the territory, someone who can take you to the best parts of the jungle while guiding you safely through the dangers. You need a guide.

Jesus is like a guide. He knows His way through life's jungle better than anyone. He wants to show you His favorite sights, places you could never find on your own. Getting to those places means passing through some pretty tough parts of the jungle, but He's an excellent guide and those who stick close to Him can make it past the dangers.

Trust Walk   Lead your child on a trust walk. You do this by blindfolding her and then leading her by the arm. Because she can't see, she has to rely on your guidance to keep her from falling or bumping into things. After several minutes of this, switch places and let her guide you.

Afterwards, talk about the experience: Ask, "How did you feel? Were you frightened? Did following get easier as time went on?" Then talk about Jesus: "How does Jesus act as a guide? Why can you trust Him? Why should you follow Him as your guide? If you follow Jesus the Guide, will you ever run into trouble? How can you learn to trust Him more as your guide?"

Self-Portraits

For this God is our God for ever and ever;
    he will be our guide even to the end.
(Psalm 48:14)

I guide you in the way of wisdom
    and lead you along straight paths.
When you walk, your steps will not be
    hampered; when you run, you will not
    stumble.   (Proverbs 4:12)

21 ◆ God Is Like an Heir
Make a Will

. . . but in these last days he has spoken to us by his Son, whom he appointed heir of all things, and through whom he made the universe. (Hebrews 1:2)

In one sense, giving your life to Jesus is like putting Him in your will. When you die, others may get your *stuff*—house, car, lawn mower, Beatles albums—but He gets *you*. And He's thrilled! He finally gets to take you home to be with Him forever. God doesn't *have* to claim His inheritance—He *chooses* to accept you.

Paul puts it this way in Ephesians 1:18: "I pray also that the eyes of your heart may be enlightened in order that you may know the hope to which He has called you, *the riches of His glorious inheritance* in the saints . . . [my italics]." God inherits *you*—and He considers it *rich and glorious*.

Make a Will Help your child write a will. It doesn't have to be official, just a list of possessions and who the child would like to give them to. Let the last beneficiary be God, and the bequest is the child's eternal life. Explain: "When you become a follower of Jesus, you give yourself to Him. When you die, He gets what is left—your soul."

Ask: "Why does God want to inherit us?"

Self-Portraits

> *The* LORD *will inherit Judah as his portion in the holy land and will again choose Jerusalem.*   (Zechariah 2:12)

> *So he became as much superior to the angels as the name he has inherited is superior to theirs.*   (Hebrews 1:4)

22 ♦ God Is Like a Hen

(Try to) Pet a Chicken

. . . how often I have longed to gather your children together, as a hen gathers her chicks under her wings, but you were not willing! (Jesus, Luke 13:34)

Wait a minute: God is like a *hen?*

But isn't a hen a female chicken? Isn't chicken the main ingredient in McNuggets, and isn't "Chicken!" an expression used to describe a coward? Isn't the chicken the butt of all jokes pertaining to crossing a particular road? And do they, or do they not, have heads that bob like something that belongs in the back window of a '65 Impala? All true, but that's not the whole story.

The moment you threaten a hen's chicks, this humble bird with the bobbing head and silly walk is transformed into a storm of wings and feathers, riveting beak, scratching claws, and ear-shattering squawking. If she succeeds in stopping your invasion, she gathers her chicks about her and spreads her wings in protection. The message is clear: if you want one of her chicks, you'll have to go through her to get it. And that's a good picture of how God protects us.

Try to Pet a Chicken   Visit a petting zoo or a farm with free-range chickens. Together with your child, watch how a hen looks after her chicks. Carefully approach her chicks to see the hen's reaction. She's not as worried about you as she is of a cat or dog, so she probably won't fly into a rage as she would with a more natural predator. If hens with chicks aren't available, observe any mother animal with her young.

Talk about what you've seen. Ask your child: "Do the chicks feel safer knowing their mom is watching over them? Do you think they're ever tired of having her be so protective? How can she be so angry with us for trying to get one of her children, and yet so loving toward her chicks?"

Talk about God the Hen. Ask your child to compare the hen to God: "How are God and the hen alike? Does God get angry with those who try to harm us? How does God cover us with His wings? Have you ever felt Him do that? How did it feel?"

Other Perspectives   *Seek Shade.*   Go for a walk on a hot day. When the heat becomes uncomfortable, sit in the shadow of a tree. Talk about the importance of shade. Ask, "How can shade protect us (from sunburn, dehydration, heat, exhaustion, enemy eyes)?" Then talk about the shadow of God's wings. Ask, "How does God protect us from danger?"

Self-Portraits

> *How priceless is your unfailing love!*
> *Both high and low among men*
>   *find refuge in the shadow of your*
> *wings.*   (Psalm 36:7)

> *Have mercy on me, O God, have mercy on*
> *me,*
>   *for in you my soul takes refuge.*
> *I will take refuge in the shadow of your wings*
>   *until the disaster has passed.*
> (Psalm 57:1)

> *He will cover you with his feathers,*
>   *and under his wings you will find refuge;*
> *his faithfulness will be your shield and*
> *rampart.*   (Psalm 91:4)

23 ◆ God Is Like a Human

Go Back in Time

The Word became flesh and lived for a while among us.   (John 1:14)

As a real, live human being, Jesus got to experience the joys of humanity first hand: laughter, sunsets, back rubs, dinner with dessert, late-night conversations with friends around a fire; the way the air smells after rain.

But Jesus also got to taste the bitter stuff: diaper rash, stubbed toes, smashed thumbs, splinters under the fingernail, boring teachers, rejection from friends, loneliness, hatred, temptation, wicked people, hunger, thirst, murder. He's not some distant and unknowable Force who's so different from us that He can't relate. He's eaten, laughed, cried, and bled—just like you. He's been in your shoes; He *knows* what it's like.

Flashback   Children sometimes have a tough time imagining that parents were ever their age. Solution: prove that you were. Find evidence of your childhood in scrapbooks, photo albums, and keepsake boxes. Ask your child to join you for a trip into your past.

Instead of focusing on what you did at their age, try to describe how you felt, what you thought, what the world looked like to you back then. For example, when you show him your team picture from Little League, describe how you felt when you struck out in the playoffs—how bad you hurt inside, how you cried all the way home. Share your moments of triumph—what you felt, how they changed your perspective. Talk about when you messed up, when you got angry or sad.

Ask your child if he's ever felt those same feelings, and when. The goal is to reverse the empathy process. Usually you say, "Son, I know how you feel"; here you want your son to say (silently or aloud), "Dad, I know how you felt." Empathy and intimacy feed each other: understanding begets closeness, closeness begets understanding.

Now talk about Jesus. If Jesus could show us His scrapbook and photo album, He'd show pictures and tell stories of things He did and felt, and we'd say, "Wow! I know how You felt." Jesus would listen to our stories and say the same thing. Ask your child: "What are some of the frustrations Jesus had? How do you think He felt? How about His triumphs? How did those feel? Have you ever had a feeling that He couldn't relate to?"

Other Perspectives *Grandmother Tells All.*
Let your child interview your parents or siblings
about what you were like as a kid. They'll volunteer
stories you might not tell yourself, but you'll look a
lot more human to your kid once he hears them.

Self-Portraits

> *For we do not have a high priest who is
> unable to sympathize with our weaknesses, but
> we have one who has been tempted in every
> way, just as we are—yet was without sin. Let
> us then approach the throne of grace with
> confidence, so that we may receive mercy and
> find grace to help us in our time of
> need.*   (Hebrews 4:15, 16)

24 ◆ God Is Like an Inventor
Make a Miniature World

You made the heavens, even the highest heavens, and all their starry host, the earth and all that is on it, the seas and all that is in them. (Nehemiah 9:6)

Have you ever created a world? A hundred times. As a child you created worlds with tinker toys, troll dolls, and Tonka trucks. You invented towns and countries in your mind and then built them with blocks, Lego blocks, and Lincoln Logs. You inherited this knack for creating stuff from your Father, who's best known for inventing the universe.

Make a World You can help your child get in touch with the inventive side of God by inventing your own world together. Set it up like this: God is forming a planet on the other side of the universe, and He wants the two of you to name the planet and design it for Him. Right now it's completely covered with water—you have to tell him where to put the land. It's smaller than earth, with enough room for three or four small continents.

Draw two large circles on poster board to represent the two hemispheres. Now decide where to put the continents. Draw their shapes and name them. Add islands if you like. Then, using assorted colored pens, create the geography: indicate mountains, deserts, plains, rivers, lakes—whatever you want. Decide on political borders: Is there just one government or several countries? Draw the borders, give names to the countries. Now decide where the people will live. Where are the cities, towns, and farmlands?

You can stop there or continue by inventing the kinds of plants and animals that live there, the climates and seasons, and what the people look like. When you're finished, talk about the experience. Was it fun? Hard? Ask, "How would you feel if the people who live on your planet started messing up all your work—killing off the animals, spoiling rivers, cutting down all the forests?"

Talk about God the Inventor: "Do you think God had fun when He created the universe? How did He decide what went where? Do you think it bothers Him when we mess up His invention? How does it make Him feel? Does He want us to be inventors like Him, or does He prefer us to leave things as they are?

Self-Portraits

> *But ask the animals, and they will teach you,*
>   *or the birds of the air, and they will tell you;*
>   *or speak to the earth, and it will teach you,*
>   *or let the fish of the sea inform you.*
> *Which of all these does not know*
>   *that the hand of the LORD has done*
> *this?*   (Job 12:7–9)

> *The earth is the LORD'S, and everything in it,*
>   *the world, and all who live in it;*
> *for he founded it upon the seas*
>   *and established it upon the*
> *waters.*   (Psalm 24:1, 2)

> *In the beginning you laid the foundations of*
> *the earth,*
>   *and the heavens are the work of your*
> *hands.*   (Psalm 102:25)

> *For every house is built by someone, but God*
> *is the builder of everything.*
> (Hebrews 3:4)

25 ◆ God Is Like a Jealous Lover
Read a Love Story

Do not worship any other god, for the LORD, whose name is Jealous, is a jealous God.   (Exodus 34:14)

The book of Hosea is a love story. At first you think it's just about a guy named Hosea, a girl named Gomer, and the children she bore—Jezreel, Lo-Ruhamah, and Lo-Ammi (you can imagine *their* first day at school). But then you realize it's also a love story about a guy named God, a girl named Israel, and the children *she* bore—Sin, Rebellion, and Unfaithfulness.

God is a jealous lover. He hates it when we set Him aside to pursue other loves. After all, He's sworn himself to be *our* lover—He's made no secret promises to potatoes or parakeets. As our lover, He's chosen to carry out His dreams through us. If we intend to be faithful, we've got to live our dreams through Him.

Read about Love   Read the first three chapters of the book of Hosea together. It's not quite like a modern romance novel. It's well-written for one thing, and much shorter for another. When you're finished, talk about the first love story—Hosea and Gomer: "Why was Hosea jealous? What did he do about it? Why did Gomer leave Hosea to love other men? Do you think she felt bad about it? Did she think about how it was hurting Hosea? What made Hosea take Gomer back?"

Then talk about the second love story—God and Israel: "Why did God get jealous? What did he do about it? Why did Israel abandon God? What made God take Israel back?"

Now talk about God's jealous love for us: "What things could you do that might make God jealous? Why would he be jealous? How does it make you feel to know that God loves you so much he can't stand it when you don't put him first?"

Self-Portraits

> *You shall not bow down to them or worship them; for I, the LORD your God, am a jealous God, punishing the children for the sin of the fathers to the third and fourth generation of those who hate me.*   (Exodus 20:5)

> *For the LORD your God is a consuming fire, a jealous God.*   (Deuteronomy 4:24)

26 ◆ God Is Like a Judge
Go to Court

And the heavens proclaim his righteousness, for God himself is judge. (Psalm 50:6)

You hear a lot about justice from your kids, at least as it applies to how others treat them. It's *me*-justice: *I* didn't do it, *I* don't deserve it, it's not fair for *me*. The Bible talks about justice too, but mostly it's *you*-justice—the kind you do for others. Judges are commissioned to administer this kind of justice. Their job is to sift out the grains of truth from the sandstorm of fiction, exaggeration, and half-truth, and then do the fair thing, no matter how painful it is.

Getting to the truth is no simple task. Thanks to God's habit of making us all unique, any two people witnessing the same occurrence are bound to see it differently. So a courtroom judge has to hear everyone describe her version and then try to imagine what *really* happened. One of the reasons why Judge God is so fair is that He doesn't have to rely on the testimony of witnesses. He sees everything and therefore knows all the facts. He also sees what's in our hearts, and so He knows the motive behind every action. He knows the truth and judges us accordingly.

Court Date You can help your child see God as a fair judge by taking him to a courtroom. Jury trials are seldom as exciting as they're portrayed on TV (unless *you're* the one being tried), but if you check the docket at the courthouse you may be able to catch part of a felony trial. Stay long enough to point out the various characters in the drama, to see a witness being sworn in, and to watch how the judge directs the proceedings.

Outside the courtroom, talk with your child about the role of a judge. Ask, "Why do people stand when she enters the room? Why does she wear a robe and sit higher than everyone else? Why do people address her *honor* rather than *her?* How does she know people are telling the truth? Do you think she feels sorry for people? Does she feel bad when she sentences someone to prison? If you were on trial for something, what kind of judge would you want?"

Now talk about Judge God: "How does He know when people are telling the truth? Does God treat people unfairly?"

Other Perspectives   *The Honorable Judge God, Presiding.*   Encourage your child to "approach the bench"—to stand before the Judge and tell Him her story. Read together 1 John 1:9: "If we confess our sins, he is faithful and just and will forgive us our sins and purify us from all unrighteousness."

Act Justly.   Micah 6:8 tells us "to act justly." Ask your child to think of a circumstance where someone wasn't treated justly (e.g., blamed for something he didn't do, denied the chance to defend himself). Who or what stood in the way of justice? Is there something your child could do to help justice prevail the next time that kind of situation occurs?

Self-Portraits

> *Now let the fear of the Lord be upon you.*
> *Judge carefully, for with the Lord our God*
> *there is no injustice or partiality or*
> *bribery.*   (2 Chronicles 19:7)

> *The Almighty is beyond our reach and exalted*
> *in power;*
>   *in his justice and great righteousness,*
> *He does not oppress.*   (Job 37:23)

27 ◆ God Is Like a King

Hold a Coronation

I am the Lord, your Holy One, Israel's Creator, your King. (Isaiah 43:15)

If as a child you were ever left in the care of an older sibling, you know what it's like to be ruled by a king or queen. The rules of monarchy are simple:

- The king owns everything in the kingdom.
- If he lets you have anything, it's a favor, not a right.
- If the king tells you to do something and you refuse, he can have your head.

These rules sound oppressive to those of us raised on the promises of life, liberty and the pursuit of happiness, yet they were the principles of virtually all governments worldwide a couple hundred years ago (and the status quo in a few countries to this day). The characteristics of a monarchy are important in understanding how God rules the world. God is not the President of Presidents, Prime Minister Eternal, or Chairman of the Universe. He's King. Which means:

- King God owns everything. He is the landlord, the master, the owner.
- King God lets us use His possessions on His behalf. We are God's slaves, stewards, servants, and one day we'll be called to account for what we did with them.
- If King God tells us to do something and we refuse, He can punish us as rebellious subjects.

What makes God a *good* king is how He treats His subjects. He's wise, generous, just, merciful, protective, quick to listen, slow to anger, and takes His greatest pleasure in seeing us happy. He loves us so much He's adopted us as His sons and daughters so we can live in His palace forever. Hail the King!

King for an Evening   To let your child understand what King God is like, crown him king (or her, queen) of your house for one evening. Make a paper crown with his name on it, give him a broom handle for a scepter. Explain that he's the ruler of the house and the family are his subjects: he's to decide about dinner, who's to prepare it, the evening entertainment, and so on. (You may want to explain that his siblings will get their moment in the throne on subsequent evenings, and so he'll get to taste his own tyranny if he gets too mean.) Set a time when the crown comes off and the family returns to "parent rule."

When your child's reign is over, talk about how he

felt being king. Was it fun? Difficult? Was he tempted
to take advantage of his subjects? What qualities
make for a good subject? How does a king keep his
subjects happy? What are the differences between a
good king and a bad one?

Now talk about King God: Ask, "How is God king
of the universe? Is He a good king? In what ways?
How are you doing as His subject? What's something
you can be doing now to be a better subject?"

Self-Portraits

*The Lord will reign for ever and
ever.*   (Exodus 15:18)

*How awesome is the Lord Most High,
    the great King over all the earth! He
subdued nations under us,
    peoples under our feet.*   (Psalm 47:2, 3)

*Now to the King eternal, immortal, invisible,
the only God, be honor and glory for ever and
ever. Amen*   (1 Timothy 1:17).

28 ◆ God Is Like a Lamb
Sacrifice Something

Look, the Lamb of God, who takes away the sin of the world! (John 1:29)

The Jews were told by God to take animals of great value and kill them to "pay" for their sins. This reminded them that sin was "expensive"—it hurt God deeply, and stood in the way of making Israel a great and powerful nation. Animal sacrifice also showed them how filthy and wasteful sin was because the sacrifice required wasting a beautiful and innocent life to cover the selfishness of the guilty.

God was very specific about the types of animals He wanted for payment. He wouldn't allow people to offer up their "discards"—old or lame animals that had little value—He was God Almighty, not a beggar in the street. One of the most expensive sacrifices they had to make was that of a year-old lamb with no marks or defects. This meant that they'd have to watch carefully over the best lambs and, just when these perfect lambs were getting old enough to earn their keep in meat, wool, or breeding, give them to God. Doing so was a real sacrifice.

In the same way, Jesus was a sacrificial lamb: a

beautiful and innocent life taken to pay for our self-ishness. It was a sacrifice so expensive, God was the only one who could afford the price (hence, Lamb of *God)*—and the payment killed him. It was a sacrifice so perfect that it covered the payment on all sins that would ever be committed throughout time. Which is good news for year-old lambs, and *great* news for humans of all ages.

Sacrifice   Help your child understand the nature of God's sacrifice by encouraging him to make a sac-rifice himself. Tell him you'd like to make a pile of stuff to donate to an organization such as the Salva-tion Army, first by helping him pick out stuff in his room and then by having him help you pick out stuff from yours. Together go through his closet, shelves, and drawers and pull out all the clothing, toys, and games he no longer needs.

When you've finished making his donation pile, say something like this: "It's great that you're willing to donate this stuff because they work with families who can't afford new clothes and toys, and this will really help them. But it's also doing *you* a favor be-cause you don't have much use for the stuff any-more; it was just taking up space. A real sacrifice is painful because it means giving up something of great value to you. I'd like to see you make that kind of a sacrifice. I'll help you make it, and then we can go in and do the same thing with my things. Do you think you can do it?"

Help him pick one of his favorite possessions to put on the donation pile. It's important that you not force him to do it—you don't want to embitter him toward the idea of giving. If he firmly refuses, just move on to your room. If he picks out something to give, ask him what he likes about the item and why it's so hard to give up. Thank him for doing it, then head over to your room and start over.

When you're done with your donations and sacrificial gift, pack it all up and take it right to the donation facility. On the way back, stop for ice cream and talk about Jesus the Lamb and his sacrifice of the most precious thing he had: Why did Jesus die?

29 ◆ God Is Like Life

Visit a Cemetery

*I am the resurrection and the life. He
who believes in me will live even
though he dies.*   (Jesus, John 11:25)

A man had a dream. He's standing in a dark room
when a figure appears and starts walking toward
him. As the figure gets closer, he recognizes it:
Death. There's no face, just a black, hooded cloak,
and in Death's hand is a sickle.

Fear paralyzes the man: he can't run away, can't
scream for help; he can barely even breath. Death
stops and points. The man is certain: "He's come for
me." Death raises the sickle, then swings. But before the blade touches the man, it's blocked by someone else's body. This person, whoever he is, falls
dead. Death covers the face with a shroud. Then he
turns and walks away. The man shouts, "Where are
you going?! You came for me!" But Death doesn't
even turn around; in a moment he's gone.

The man kneels at the body of the person who took
Death's blow. He lifts the shroud. He looks into the
face of a man he'd never met. He replaces the shroud
and steps back from the body, feeling sick and con-

fused. There comes a shudder from the corpse; then it sits up, then stands, then pulls the shroud from its face, like a statue making its own unveiling. But it's not a statue—the man is alive. He tears the shroud in half and tosses the shreds aside. His face is brilliant. The blood is gone; his shirt is blinding white, a scar marks his neck. He smiles and walks away.

You guessed it—this wasn't a dream. It's an allegory of what actually happened to *you*. You're the one Death came for. You're the one Death swung at. But Jesus stepped in and took your place. He took your death and died for you. It's like he stole the period from the end of your sentence And he put it in the . middle of his so that you never have to end; he's deathproofed you—the grave has no power to stop your life, and you are now free to live forever . . . no question mark, no exclamation point, and absolutely, no period

Where, O death, is your victory?
Where, O death, is your sting?   (1 Corinthians 15:55)

Cemetery Visit   God gives life by taking away death. To help your child understand how God is like life itself, visit a cemetery. Walk quietly among the graves; visit the gravesite of a loved one if you wish. After a while, sit down on a bench and give your child an opportunity to tell you what he's thinking. Ask, "Is this scary for you? Is it sad? Why?" Get both your and your child's feelings out in the open so you'll feel more comfortable about the setting.

Then turn the conversation toward death in general: "Why do people have to die? What happens to them when they do? Do they cease to exist, or do their minds continue on somehow?" To know whether or not there's life after death, it seems we'd have to talk to someone who's been there and come back. Can you think of anyone who's managed to do that? Why did Jesus go through all that pain and trouble?

Now talk about God's promise of a deathproof life. "Why does God want us to live forever? How can we be sure that He'll do what He says? Is there anything we need to do to hold up our end of the promise?"

Self-Portraits

> *O LORD, you brought me up from the grave;*
>   *you spared me from going down into the*
> *pit.*   (Psalm 30:3)

> *I tell you the truth, whoever hears my word*
> *and believes him who sent me has eternal life*
> *and will not be condemned; he has crossed*
> *over from death to life.*   (Jesus, John 5:24)

30 ◆ God Is Like a Lifeguard

Practice Lifesaving

He reached down from on high and took hold of me; he drew me out of deep waters. (2 Samuel 22:17)

My friend Lanny prints and sells T-shirts. He makes a tanktop with the word LIFEGUARD printed across the front. It looks like the typical lifeguard shirt, until you read what is printed in smaller letters just above it: GOD IS MY.

It's not only a fun shirt—it's an accurate picture of God. To understand how God acts as our lifeguard, you need to understand what lifeguards are supposed to do.

Lifeguards have two duties. The first is to *guard* us from danger; the second is to *save* us if we get into trouble. The first duty compels them to post huge signs that say NO HORSEPLAY and to scream, "No running!" Without this duty to guard you from trouble, they could scream things like, "Go ahead and run—I have a first aid kit."

The second duty, to *save* us if we get into trouble, is just as important. It is their job to rescue us—even when we've ignored their advice and played with horses or slipped while running.

Lifeguard God performs these same two duties all the time. He guards us from all sorts of hazards, and He saves us when we get into trouble.

Hit the Water Take your child and one of his friends to the pool or beach. Tell them to pretend that they've just been hired as lifeguards: their first responsibility is to identify any hazards, and then to make up a list of rules to try to stop people from being hurt by them.

Unless you've discovered a secret swimming hole, a list of rules is probably posted nearby. With the kids, read the list and figure out the logic behind each of the rules. Any unnecessary rules? Any that should be added?

Next, get in the water and, if you know how, show the children some lifesaving skills. If you don't know the basics well enough to teach them, perhaps a lifeguard could help. When everyone is ready to rest a while, talk about Lifeguard God.

Here are some discussion ideas: "As head lifeguard for the planet, has God identified any hazards we should look out for? Has He posted a list of them anywhere? What's on that list? Has He made up any rules that are unnecessary?"

Ask, "If you do something you know is dangerous (shoplifting, skateboarding in busy parking lots), will

God still help you? How? If you obey all the rules, are you safe? Can you think of examples where God reaches out to save people from situations they didn't cause?"

Continue, "Can you think of an example in your own life where Lifeguard God guarded you from trouble or saved you from a bad situation? If He were sitting in a lifeguard tower right here, and He was about to warn you about some hazard in your life now, what would He say to you?

Other Perspectives *Give a Whistle.* If you've tried the above activity, you can give your child a whistle on a lanyard to remind him of the picture of God as his lifeguard.

Like a Bodyguard. A bodyguard is like a terrestrial lifeguard. His duties are to protect and to rescue the person he's guarding. Ask your child: "How is God like a personal bodyguard?"

Assistant Lifeguard. God can use each of us to help guard the lives of those around us. Ask your child to explain how he would be a lifeguard to a friend in each of these situations: a bad home life, a problem with drugs, in trouble with the law, being picked on at school.

31 ◆ God Is Like a Light
Turn Out the Lights

I am the light of the world. Whoever follows me will never walk in darkness, but will have the light of life.
(Jesus, John 8:12)

People aren't afraid of the dark—it's what's hidden in it that they worry about.

What hides in the dark? Lots of things: snakes, spiders, lizards, roaches, scorpions, bats, lions and tigers and bears (oh my), robbers, murderers, terrorists, monsters, aliens, ghosts, Bigfoot, Godzilla, King Kong, and the bogeyman.

That is just what's *outside* the body. Darkness on the inside is even scarier: evil thoughts, worries, fears; those nagging questions about death, value, purpose, love, failure. Life can seem like a room with no lights where you wander around blindly bumping into things. If you're lucky, you bump into good things. If you're unlucky, you bump into trouble.

The good news is that God has entered the room and switched on a light. He lights up our paths so we won't stumble. He shines into our brains (for me it's like a fog lamp) to help us make good decisions, to think clearly, to avoid heading into trouble. When we run into trouble anyway, He shines into our hearts, giving us the reason to go on.

Sit in the Dark   Here is a nighttime activity that
will help your child understand how God is like a light. Tell your child that the two of you are going to do an experiment with light. Then remove the shade from a table lamp, set the lamp on the floor in the middle of the room, and turn it on. Draw the blinds, and turn off all the lights in the house. Sit next to each other beside the lamp (you may wish to reassure him that you're not going to scare him).

Tell your child you are going to switch the light off for a while but that you'll be there with him and will ask him some questions. Switch off the lamp. While sitting in the darkness, talk about light. Ask, "What does light do for us (lets us see, makes colors, illuminates dangers, takes away our fears of the unknown)? What don't you like about the dark? How does it make you feel?"

Now switch on the lamp. Ask, "How do you feel now? Why do you feel better when the light is on? How is God like a light? How does God take away fear? Does God turn His light on and off, or is it on all the time?"

Other Perspectives *Junior Lights.* In Matthew 5:14–16, Jesus claims that we are lights too. Read the verses together and figure out what we are supposed to do about it.

Self-Portraits

> *He is like the light of morning at sunrise*
> *on a cloudless morning,*
> *like the brightness after rain*
> *that brings the grass from the earth.*
> (2 Samuel 23:4)

> *The LORD is my light and my salvation—*
> *whom shall I fear?*   (Psalm 27:1)

> *Your word is a lamp to my feet*
> *and a light for my path.*
> (Psalm 119:105)

> *In him was life, and that life was the light of*
> *men.*   (John 1:4)

> *I have come into the world as a light, so that*
> *no one who believes in me should stay in*
> *darkness.*   (Jesus, John 12:46)

32 ◆ God Is Like a Lion

Read a Lion's Tale

Do not weep! See, the Lion of the tribe of Judah, the Root of David, has triumphed. (Revelation 5:5)

The picture of Jesus as a lion is a popular one, but you have to get all the way to the back of the Bible to find the only reference to it. Nonetheless, it's a wonderful picture, conveying two seemingly opposite impressions at the same time: beauty and terror.

Read The best illustration of Jesus as a lion is in C.S. Lewis's classic children's fantasy work, The Chronicles of Narnia. The seven-book series takes you to Narnia, a world of kings and castles, talking animals, and a Christlike Lion named Aslan, son of the Emperor-Beyond-the-Sea. Each book is a complete story in itself, so you don't have to read the whole series.

The best way to read The Chronicles is by starting with book one: *The Lion, the Witch and the Wardrobe.* The story is exciting and fast-moving, so it's lots of fun to read aloud. Read a chapter a night, or gather around the fireplace and read several in one sitting. The parallels between Aslan and Jesus are numerous, so you'll have no problem painting a picture of God as a lion.

33 ◆ God Is Like a Listener

Listen Quietly

Before they call I will answer; while they are still speaking I will hear. (Isaiah 65:24)

Have you ever been talking on the phone when, in the middle of telling your story, you realize you haven't heard an "uh huh" or "really?" in the last minute or so? You start to wonder if the listener is there. Maybe she's set the phone down to turn on the TV or to make tuna salad. Or maybe she's still there, but not *there:* opening the mail, filing a nail, or drawing a moustache on the realtor's notepad photo.

Have you ever been talking to God and wondered the same thing? Maybe He's tired of hearing about your problems and requests. Or He's bored. Maybe he has too many people talking to Him at once—He's kicking Himself for creating a round world because it means it's always bedtime prayer time *somewhere* on the globe. This is silly conjecture, of course, but it brings up an important question: *When you're pouring out your heart to God, is He really listening?*

If the Bible is true, the answer is yes. God knows the frustration of talking to someone who isn't listening—we do it to Him every day—so He promises again and again to listen to us whenever we call. And sometimes, if you stay quiet long enough, God the Listener becomes God the Voice.

Quiet Listening   Introduce your child to the picture of God the Listener by teaching her to listen quietly. Take the phone off the hook, turn off TVs, stereos, and other noise makers, and sit together quietly for a couple of minutes. Take note of the sounds you hear—the whir of the refrigerator, the house settling, your own breathing, a neighbor's door slam, a distant shout, a plane overhead.

Afterward, talk about the things you heard. Were there any noises you've never noticed before? Were there any you didn't recognize? Did you feel silly sitting still? Did you feel uncomfortable?

Talk about God the Listener: Ask, "Did God hear all those sounds? Does He hear every noise in the world? How can He hear two noises or voices at the same time? How many people can He hear at once? When we pray to Him, does He hear all our prayers, or just the important ones? How can you tell if He's listening? Does He answer back? How do you listen to God?"

Other Perspectives   *Silent Times.*   Other settings are good for quiet moments: a park, forest, beach, near a stream. Be quiet at different times of the day: sunrise, sunset, in place of grace before a meal.

Eye Listening.   Hold a silent family meal. From the moment you sit at the table until the meal is over, no talking. To communicate, use gestures; to listen, watch.

Self-Portraits

What other nation is so great as to have their gods near them the way the LORD *our God is near us whenever we pray to him?*
(Deuteronomy 4:7)

You hear, O LORD, *the desire of the afflicted;*
    you encourage them, and you listen to their
cry.   (Psalm 10:17)

The eyes of the LORD *are on the righteous*
    and his ears are attentive to their cry.
(Psalm 34:15)

34 ◆ God Is Like a Messenger
Deliver a Message

Then suddenly the Lord you are seeking will come to his temple; the messenger of the covenant, whom you desire, will come. (Malachi 3:1)

Let's say you had an important message for someone who just happened to live on the other side of the planet. How would you communicate? You can't call, because she doesn't have a telephone. You could send a letter, but the mail delivery between here and there is too slow; it could take months, or even get lost in the mail. You could try a telegram, but that's impersonal, and there's no signature to prove that it was really you who sent it. If the message is *really* important, there's only one way to send it: deliver it yourself.

God did that when He sent Jesus the Messenger to us. The message Jesus delivered was this:

My Dear Child,
    I love you. I want you to live with Me forever. Hope to hear from you soon!

                    All My love,
                    God

I'm paraphrasing, of course. The actual message was much longer, and Jesus said many other wonderful (and disturbing) things. The point is that the message was important enough for God to deliver Himself. He knew that "Long distance is the next best thing . . . ," but He couldn't settle for *next* best. It had to be the best, and that meant face to face.

Deliver   Let your child catch the picture of Messenger Jesus by being a messenger herself. Have her prepare a surprise message she can deliver to a parent or other family member while that person is at work. For example, help her bake cookies and rehearse a birthday message for her dad. Make sure he'll be at work when you arrive. Tell her to deliver the message in person. She might say something like, "I wanted to wish you a happy birthday in person. The message was too important to say over the phone."

On the way home, ask her how it went: "Was Dad surprised? How do you think he liked the message? Do you think he will remember this?" Then talk about Messenger Jesus: "Why did Jesus come to Earth? Couldn't God have just shouted from the sky? Why is it more special to have God deliver the message in person? What was His message?"

35 ◆ God Is Like a Mom
Take a Mom Survey

As a mother comforts her child, so will I comfort you . . .   (Isaiah 66:13)

Moms wrote the book on comfort. As a kid, if I came in wet and shivering from the rain, my mother would immediately get me out of wet clothes and into a hot bath. Then Mom put my fresh clothes in the dryer so they'd be toasty hot when I put them on. And there might even be a cup of hot chocolate waiting for me in the kitchen. By the time my mother was through with me, I wasn't sure I'd ever been miserable at all.

God the Mom is like that. She takes us in from the cold, bathes us in warmth, wraps us in comfort. She lets us forget for a moment how cold the world can be.

Mom Survey   Conduct a survey following the directions for Idea 12, God is Like a Dad, only use the Mom Survey.

Mom Survey

What are the 3
most important responsibilities of a mom?

1. _____

2. _____

3. _____

What's your favorite part of being a mom?

_____

_____

_____

What's your *least* favorite thing about being a mom?

_____

_____

_____

36 ◆ God Is Like a Party Host
Check Out the Church Party

I have come that they may have life, and have it to the full.
(Jesus, John 10:10)

Once upon a time, God decided to throw a party. He sent out invitations to His special friends. He made all the preparations and spared no expense. When it came time for the party, none of those He invited showed up. Some had other plans, some were too busy with work and family obligations, some stayed home to watch wrestling on TV. With all this food, a band, and decorations about to go to waste, God said, "Fine! If those I invited don't want to come, I'm going to invite *everyone*—complete strangers, bums off the street, anyone who wants to come."

The party is life with God. The guest list is no longer exclusive. Anyone invited can come and join in the celebration.

Church Party One of the reasons we go to church is to celebrate life with God. Explain to your child that church is kind of like a party. Talk about your own church: What kind of party is it?

The Guest List.   Who is invited to your church? Can anyone show up? Or are there only certain kinds of people who are accepted? Jesus invites everyone to the party, no one is too "uncool" for Him.

The Celebration.   The fact that we can actually live forever is something to get excited about! Does your church ever celebrate that? You don't have to wear party hats, crack open a piñata, or play pin the tail on the donkey, but does going to church ever seem like a celebration? God the Host fills our lives with joy and laughter.

The Host.   Does it seem like the ministers and teachers at your church are excited about holding a celebration? Or are they just doing it because they have to? God the Host wants to please us. He threw this party of life for us.

37 ♦ God Is Like a Potter

Play with Clay

*Yet, O LORD, you are our Father. We
are the clay, you are the potter; we are
all the work of your hand.*
(Isaiah 64:8)

Have you ever watched a potter at work? It's hard to
decide what's more beautiful: the vessel formed from
a lump of clay, or the dance the potter's hands perform to create it. She makes it look easy, but throwing a pot is difficult and delicate work. To make a
pot, everything has to be right: the consistency of the
clay, the wetness of her hands, the speed of the
wheel, the thickness of the pot. If something is
wrong, the pot collapses in her hands.

Even if she forms a beautiful pot, an air bubble
hidden in the clay can explode while being fired, de-
stroying her work—and everything else in the kiln. If
her work survives the wheel and the kiln, the finished work of art is so delicate it will shatter if
dropped or hit.

God is like a potter. He works long and hard to
shape us into intricate and delicate forms. He carefully molds us into vessels that are both beautiful and

useful. When He's finished forming us, our lives are as fragile as a clay pot.

Clay Play   Get some clay from an art supply store. You should be able to find the kind that can harden without a kiln. Don't bother trying to use a potter's wheel for this activity—they're hard to work with and frustrating to learn on. Instead, form bowls or other small objects using your hands. While you and your child are working, talk about God the Potter.

Self-Portraits

> *You turn things upside down, as if the potter were thought to be like the clay! Shall what is formed say to him who formed it, "He did not make me"? Can the pot say of the potter, "He knows nothing"?*   (Isaiah 29:16)

> *Does not the potter have the right to make out of the same lump of clay some pottery for noble purposes and some for common use?*   (Romans 9:21)

38 ◆ God Is Like a Priest
Make a Confession

For we do not have a high priest who is unable to sympathize with our weaknesses, but we have one who has been tempted in every way, just as we are—yet was without sin. Let us then approach the throne of grace with confidence, so that we may receive mercy and find grace to help us in our time of need. (Hebrews 4:15,16)

Priests are spiritual middlemen, standing between a squeaky-clean God and dirty-behind-the-ears humans. In the Old Testament, priests offered the sacrifices and performed the rituals on behalf of the rest of the people. Because God was a stickler for detail, these middlemen had to be trained carefully and kept pure for their sacred duties.

Then along came Jesus, the ideal middleman. He's fully human, so He's qualified to speak for the human party; and He's fully God, so He represents the heavenly realm. He's the perfect priest, literally.

Here's a play-by-play look at how this new arrangement works: When you sin, you go to Jesus the Priest and confess (i.e., you admit your selfishness, express sorrow for disobeying God, ask for forgiveness). As a fellow human, He identifies with your struggle and hurts *with* you. He turns to God the Father and says, "I know this person, and I know what she's done. I've made the payment for her sin, and I wish to forgive her." God says, "Do it," then Jesus says to you: "Your sin is covered, you are forgiven." You're clean.

In religious talk, Jesus the Priest is our confessor, intercessor, atoner and forgiver, all wrapped in one. When you have business with God, Jesus is the one to talk to.

Confess   Here's an activity that can help your child understand the role of Jesus the Priest. To prepare, you'll need some flash paper, which is paper that burns completely when ignited, leaving no ashes or scraps. You can buy this wherever magic tricks are sold.

Both you and your child will need a sheet of flash paper. Explain that you both are to write notes of confession to Jesus: list your sins and ask Jesus to forgive you. After writing the notes fold them in half and put them in a bowl. Explain why you've written the notes to Jesus: because He's human and understands how we're tempted and can relate to our struggles. Explain that when we confess our sins to Him, He then goes to God the Father *for* us. God agrees that the sin was already paid for with Christ's sacrifice. Jesus then erases the sin and tells us we're forgiven.

Now light a match and toss it into the bowl. The paper, along with the sins, will vanish in a bright flash. Take a moment to thank God for His forgiveness. Talk about the experience: "Do you feel forgiven? How do you know if you really are? Do you think God photocopied our notes before they were destroyed? Why does God forgive us? Why do we talk to God through Jesus?"

Other Perspectives   *Clean Slate.*   If you can't find flash paper, you can use regular paper and burn it in the fireplace or sink, or use a dry-erase board (wipe it, don't burn it), or use a word processor and just delete the document without saving it.

Self-Portraits

> *If we confess our sins, he is faithful and just and will forgive us our sins and purify us from all unrighteousness.*   (1 John 1:9)

39 ◆ God Is Like Rain

Go Puddle-Jumping

He will be like rain falling on a mown field, like showers watering the earth. (Psalm 72:6)

Rain is nature's way of taking a bath. It cleans the air, washes dust from the leaves, rinses off rocks and grass, flushes out streams. Rain makes the air smell better—or maybe it just washes away the things that make air smell bad. Rain makes seeds sprout, flowers bloom, and brown hillsides turn green.

God is like rain. He washes off the dirt and grime in our lives, He makes breathing fun. He refreshes us and brings new joy to our tired lives. He does it just by letting His grace fall on us.

Jump Puddles Take your kid puddle-jumping.* Put on raincoats (or cut head and arm holes in a couple of plastic trash bags) and head outside. Try to catch raindrops in your mouth. What do they taste like? Race sticks in the gutter. Try to stomp all the

---

* Contrary to what our moms told us, you don't catch a cold or flu by getting wet. You get into trouble when you stay wet too long and your body gets exhausted trying to keep warm: this lowers your body's defenses.

water out of a puddle. Stand on a street corner and wait for cars to drive through and drench you. Take a shower beneath a rain gutter.

Go to a playground. Glide down a wet slide. Try out the swings. Put your feet down and waterski across the puddle beneath the swing. Run and slide through a puddle in the grass. Hold a contest to see who can slide farther.

When you've had enough puddle jumping, head home and change into dry clothes. If the weather suits, light a fire in the fireplace and serve hot apple cider or hot chocolate. Talk about your adventure and how God is like rain.

Self-Portraits

Let my teaching fall like rain
and my words descend like dew,
like showers on new grass,
like abundant rain on tender
plants. (Deuteronomy 32:2)

Let us acknowledge the LORD;
let us press on to acknowledge him.
As surely as the sun rises
he will appear,
he will come to us like the winter rains,
like the spring rains that water the
earth. (Hosea 6:3)

40 ◆ God Is Like a Rescue Worker

Rehearse a Rescue

For he has rescued us from the dominion of darkness and brought us into the kingdom of the Son he loves. (Colossians 1:13)

A paramedic studies, trains, and rehearses long and hard for one job: to save lives. He saves babies, old people, friends, total strangers, handsome people, ugly people, heros, and criminals. It's his job.

That's Jesus's job too. He doesn't save just the rich or the good-looking or those with perfect church-attendance records. He saves anyone who calls out for Him.

Rescue Rehearsal To help your child see God as a rescue worker, give him the chance to be one himself. If he's old enough, take a first-aid course with him through your local Red Cross. Together you can practise the Heimlich maneuver to save someone from choking and how to perform rescue breathing. You will learn how to stop the bleeding from a major cut, what not to do with a back or neck injury, and what to do if someone swallows poison.

Conduct a family fire drill. Perhaps an older child can figure out how to help a younger sibling in case of fire. Demonstrate what the smoke alarm sounds like, show where the fire extinguisher is and how to use it, how to feel a door for heat before opening it, and how to stay low to minimize breathing smoke.

Talk about why it is important to know these things. Ask, "If you had the chance to rescue someone, would you do it? Why? Would you risk your own life to save someone else's? Why do some people such as firefighters and paramedics choose to make a living out of rescuing people?"

Now ask your child to compare God to a rescue worker. Ask, "How does God save people? What danger does He save them from? Why does He do it? Does He ever risk His own life to save someone? When someone is rescued by God, how does He feel?"

Other Perspectives *Ask a Rescuer Why.* Call a fire station or ambulance company and ask if you and your child can stop by for a few minutes to interview a paramedic. Go to the station and talk to the paramedic about his work. Ask why he chose this profession; what he enjoys most; what's the worst part.

41 ◆ God Is Like a Rock

Go Climbing

*From the ends of the earth I call to
you, I call as my heart grows faint;
lead me to the rock that is higher
than I.*   (Psalm 61:2)

A tsunami is a giant sea wave formed by an earthquake or volcanic eruption. In places like Hawaii,
where tsunami warnings aren't uncommon, there's
only one safe place to go—up. When the warning
goes out, friends and neighbors meet on the hills and
clifftops surrounding the town. If the tsunami hits
the shore, it can wipe out anything at or near sea
level—trees, houses, an entire town.

Life has its share of tsunamis, floods, tidal waves,
and hurricanes. When these or other physical or
emotional disasters strike, it's reassuring to know
that our God is a solid and unmovable rock.

Climb a Rock Find some rocks you can climb
with your child without either of you getting into danger. Scramble around for a while, trying different
routes, exploring the cracks and crevices. When you
get to the top, sit down together for a snack. Read
the parable about the man who builds his house in

the sand and the one who builds his on the rock (Luke 6:46–49). Talk about the meaning of the parable. Ask: "How is God like a rock?"

Self-Portraits

> *The LORD lives! Praise be to my Rock!*
> *Exalted be God, the Rock, my Savior!*
> (2 Samuel 22:47)

> *He lifted me out of the slimy pit,*
> *out of the mud and mire;*
> *he set my feet on a rock*
> *and gave me a firm place to*
> *stand.* (Psalm 40:2)

> *My salvation and my honor depend on God;*
> *he is my mighty rock, my refuge.* (Psalm 62:7)

> *Trust in the LORD forever,*
> *for the LORD, the LORD, is the Rock*
> *eternal.* (Isaiah 26:4)

42 ◆ God Is Like a Roommate

Tour the House

I pray that out of his glorious riches he may strengthen you with power through his Spirit in your inner being, so that Christ may dwell in your hearts through faith. (Ephesians 3:16, 17)

When you invite Christ to be a part of your life, He comes to live in your "heart." A brilliant illustration of this idea was written by Robert Munger in a booklet called *My Heart, Christ's Home* (1954, Inter-Varsity Press), a story of a man who invited Christ to live in his heart.

When Christ moves into the man's heart, the two take a tour: they check out the library (his mind), dining room (appetites and desires), workshop (work), as well as other important rooms in his life. The man soon discovers that his new roommate has His own ideas about how these rooms ought to be used. With the man's permission, Christ transforms the man's heart, room by room, into a warm and beautiful home.

House Tour Get a copy of *My Heart, Christ's Home* to read to your child. As you read each section of the story, walk into the room of your house that corresponds with that section. You may have to improvise—a desk can act as the study, for example. As you tour the house, feel free to set the story aside to talk about the messages as they apply to your child's life. Ask her about the rooms in her own heart. What would Jesus say as He walked into *her* dining room, *her* library?

43 ◆ God Is Like a Servant
Be a Butler

Who, being in very nature God, did not consider equality with God something to be grasped, but made himself nothing, taking the very nature of a servant. (Philippians 2:6, 7)

Throughout time, governments and companies around the world have developed organizational charts with the head honcho (queen, president, dictator, grand poobah) at the top, with lesser honchos arranged at various levels beneath.

Along comes Jesus, who flips the whole thing upside down: the first will be last, the exalted will be humbled, and all sorts of other convoluted ideas about leadership. True to style, Jesus didn't stand in a pulpit and preach the virtues of servanthood. Instead, He got down on His hands and knees and washed people's feet.

Be a Butler Together with your child, serve a formal meal to the rest of the family. Dress up as formal waiters, with dress pants, white shirts, and ties. Prepare the dinner table with a tablecloth, candles, and your best dishes. Fold the napkins into strange shapes like they do at fancy restaurants. Oh yes—don't forget to make a nice meal.

Seat family members when they arrive for dinner; place napkins on their laps, pour water, serve the food, and generally hover over them during the meal. After the main course, clear the dishes and serve dessert. If you've done well, maybe you'll get a big tip.

Afterward, talk with your child about how it felt to be a servant. Then talk about God the Servant: what He's done to serve us and how He demonstrated servanthood.

Other Perspectives *Foot Bath.* It's hard to imagine Jesus getting down on His hands and knees to wash twenty-four feet in the middle of dinner! But that's what He did to teach servanthood, and you may want to try the gesture to convey the same message. The washing instructions appear in John 13:1–13.

Self-Portraits

> *"If anyone wants to be first, he must be the very last, and the servant of all."*
> (Jesus, Mark 9:35)

44 ◆ God Is Like a Shepherd
Take Care of a Pet

I am the good shepherd. The good shepherd lays down his life for the sheep. (Jesus, John 10:11)

I have no problem imagining God as a shepherd. The part I have trouble with is admitting that I'm a sheep. It's not a flattering metaphor. Sheep seem preoccupied with one thing: feeding themselves. They seem stupid, easily frightened, and prone to wandering into trouble. Okay, so the metaphor is accurate. At least there's some comfort in knowing that, if I have to play the part of a sheep, Jesus is willing to play the part of the shepherd.

Pet Care You may not have a paddock of sheep at your house, but if you have a pet, you can use it to help create the picture of God the Shepherd. Help your child fill out the chart, "Responsibilities of a Good Pet Owner."

When he's done with this chart, help him fill in the second chart, "Responsibilities of God the Shepherd."

Responsibilities of a
Good Pet Owner

Pet's name: _____ Age: _____

Type of animal: ☐ dog ☐ cat ☐ fish

☐ other _____ ☐ rabbit ☐ snake ☐ zebra

NEED	RESPON-SIBILITY	WHEN & HOW OFTEN	WHAT HAPPENS IF YOU FORGET
FOOD			
SHELTER			
HEALTH			
LOVE & ATTENTION			

Responsibilities of
God the Shepherd

Sheep's name (that's you!): _____ Age: ____

Type of sheep: ☐ ewe   ☐ ram

NEED	RESPON-SIBILITY	WHEN & HOW OFTEN	WHAT HAPPENS IF GOD FORGETS
FOOD			
SHELTER			
HEALTH			
LOVE & ATTENTION			

45 ◆ God Is Like a Shield

Stage a Newspaper Battle

The LORD is my strength and my shield; my heart trusts in him, and I am helped. (Psalm 28:7)

A shield is like a portable fortress that you can hide behind for protection in battle. Because it's portable, you can use it when you're on the offense; a fortress is strictly for defense. A shield gives a warrior more confidence because he can attack with less fear of being hurt. It doesn't make the battle a cinch—a stray arrow can hit you from the side, and a crushing blow from a sword or ax can break the arm holding the shield. Still, it makes a battle a little less dangerous.

God is like a shield. He goes with us in life, helping to protect us from attack.

Paper Battle To demonstrate the power of a shield, stage a newspaper battle in the house. You and your child each build a shield out of thick cardboard. You can make handles by poking a few holes in the right places and looping small pieces of rope through the back. Decorate the shields with paint or colored pens. If you don't care to make your own shields, you can use trash can lids.

Once you have your shields, you'll need to make your weapons. Each side gets a stack of newspapers. Make paper grenades by wadding up sheets of newspaper. Now mark off some kind of line down the middle of the room, stand on your respective sides, and start firing by throwing the soft paper wads at each other.

Play two rounds of two minutes each. Fight the first round without your shields, the second one with them. To keep score, count the number of times you manage to hit your opponent's body, or just see who has the least amount of paper on her side of the room at the end of the round.

When you've had enough, call a truce, clean up the papers, and then go wash the newspaper ink off your hands. Talk about the shields. Were they helpful? How many times were you hit without your shield? With it? Now talk about God: How is He like a shield?

Self-Portraits

My shield is God Most High,
*   who saves the upright in heart.*
(Psalm 7:10)

46 ◆ God Is Like a Teacher
Play Teacher

In a culture where the religious instructors prided themselves in delivering obtuse lectures, pointless arguments, and long-winded prayers, Jesus was a renegade teacher. He avoided long messages; instead He told colorful stories, asked plenty of questions, left people begging for more (when's the last time you wished the sermon was longer?). He was a master of multimedia, using sight, sound, taste, touch and smell to make a message unforgettable (feeding the five thousand, the Last Supper). Most important, He loved his students, and they knew it.

Professor Jesus was a master teacher. We have much to learn from what He taught *and* how He taught it.

Play Teacher   Set up a classroom at home with you as the student and your child as the teacher. Ask her to prepare a short lesson for you on a subject she knows well, such as how to use a dictionary, how to divide, state geography, the meaning of a certain Bible passage, anything she feels confident to teach.

While she's the teacher, stay in character as a stu-

274 Teaching Your Child About God

dent. You can ask lots of questions, but don't tell her how to teach and don't use this time to correct her if she makes a mistake (but if she tries to send you to the principal's office, send her to her room).

At the end of the lesson, ask her what it was like to be a teacher. Ask, "How did you feel? Was it fun? Frustrating?" Ask her to identify what makes a good teacher or a bad teacher. Then talk about Professor Jesus. Ask, "What kind of teacher was Jesus? How do you know? What teaching methods did Jesus use to get His message across? How did He treat His students?"

47 ◆ God Is Like a Team Captain
Choose Sides

But you are a chosen people, a royal priesthood, a holy nation, a people belonging to God, that you may declare the praises of him who called you out of darkness into his wonderful light.
(1 Peter 2:9)

Many of us have had this experience at one time in our lives: They're choosing teams for a game of some sort, and the two team captains are standing in front of a crowd of prospective team members. The captains alternate picking people from the crowd. They each pick their best friends on the first round, and their next best friends on round two. Then they search the crowd for the best players, each captain being accosted by a dozen waving hands and the pleas of "Pick me!"

As the crowd thins out, the kids who've been picked are obviously the lucky ones. Cries of "Pick me!" sound desperate now.

There are just a few kids left. No one bothers to beg, but on the inside you're all praying, "Don't let me be last—again." Now there are four left—a 25 percent chance. Now a one-in-three chance. Now it's fifty-fifty. Then it's just you—your pleas went unanswered.

Now the two team captains start arguing. It seems there's an uneven number of players—you're the odd one—and neither wants to get stuck with you. The loser of the argument grimaces and calls you over. Oh joy.

The Bible says that God chooses you to be on His team. So if you've ever experienced anything like the above, you may think God chooses you because He *has to:* "After all, I'm God. I'm *supposed* to pick him. It's in My contract." Or maybe you think He picks you because He's a nice God and He *feels sorry* for you: "If I don't pick him, who else will?" But it's not like that. Captain God chooses you because He *wants you.* He wants you on His team.

Last Pick   Ask your child to recall a time when he was chosen last, or nearly so. Ask him to describe what it felt like and why he was picked last. Ask him if he's ever been picked first, or nearly so, and what that felt like. Ask him why he was chosen first. Now explain that he has been picked for a team—God's team. Ask, "Why do you think God picked you? What can you do for Him, now that you are on His team?"

48 ◆ God Is Like a Tower

Get Tall

*The name of the LORD is a strong
tower; the righteous run to it and are
safe.*   (Proverbs 18:10)

When I was about ten years old I managed to talk my
big sister into taking me to the beach with her
friends for a day. As soon as we got there, I waded
out into the surf up to my waist. When I looked up, I
saw a massive wave preparing to break in front of
me. I panicked. I tried to scramble for the beach, but
the undertow pulled my feet out from under me and
started to drag me under the breaking wave. I called
out for help.

My sister's friend was standing several yards
away. Jim, who was nearly seven feet tall, ran to me,
yanked me out of the water and over the top of the
wave just as it broke. How small the wave looked
from up there. It was the same wave; the only thing
that had changed was my perspective.

God is like a tower: tall, magnificent, indestructi-
ble. His tower doesn't lean, and He doesn't even
charge admission. The view from the top convinces

you that even your biggest problem is much smaller than God.

Tall Trip   Visit a tower with your child. If you live near a big city, there's probably an observation deck in one of the tall buildings. Or just look for anything with a view: an office building, apartment tower, or mountain overlook. Talk about the feelings of being up high. Ask, "Does being up high make you feel stronger or more powerful? Is it scary? Why do people build tall buildings? How is God like a tower?"

Self-Portraits

> *From the ends of the earth I call to you,*
> *I call as my heart grows faint;*
> *lead me to the rock that is higher than I.*
> *For you have been my refuge,*
> *a strong tower against the foe.*
> (Psalm 61:2, 3)

49 ◆ God Is Like a Vine
Find a Vine

I am the vine; you are the branches. If a man remains in me and I in him, he will bear much fruit; apart from me you can do nothing.
(Jesus, John 15:5)

Grapes don't actually grow from grape vines, they grow from branches attached to the vine. The vine itself may be over a hundred years old, but the branches are new with each season.

God is like a grape vine. He doesn't grow fruit directly; He grows and nurtures good branches to bear the fruit for Him. You're one of His branches. Stay attached to Him, and He'll send you what you need to grow good fruit. Break off from God and the fruit dies, you die, and God ends up with less fruit. It's a bad deal all around. Stay connected.

Vine Find You can help your child see this botanical picture of God by showing him a real vine in action. If you can't locate a grape vine, look for some kind of berry vine. If vines are hard to find where you live, a fruit tree will do. Explain how the vine grows branches for bearing fruit. Point out how the vine nurtures the branches so they can grow strong enough to hold the weight of the fruit yet be flexible enough to survive shaking in the wind.

Look for a branch that's broken off the vine. Have your child estimate the chances that this branch will bear fruit. Now talk about God the Vine: "If God is the vine, who are the branches? What are the fruit? How do we keep growing good fruit?"

Other Perspectives   *Fruit-of-the-Vine Picnic.* Put together a picnic lunch made from grapes: peanut butter sandwiches with grape jelly, grapes, raisins, grape juice, raisin bread. Talk about how grapes grow and how God is like a vine.

50 ◆ God Is Like a Voice

Name that Voice

The voice of the LORD is powerful; the voice of the LORD is majestic.
(Psalm 29:4)

The portable audiotape recorder was invented about nineteen hundred years too late to catch God's voice on tape. If we'd gotten His voice on tape that day by the Jordan River when He said, "This is My Son . . . ," we'd know whether His voice is really as deep and echoey as it sounds in all those old movies. (A recording would almost certainly prove that He never spoke with a slight British accent, and that he never even spoke in English.)

Except for occasional tabloid reports ("God Spoke Through My Toaster—in Dutch!") we don't hear about God speaking out loud to people anymore. It was a rare thing even in biblical times. God saves His audible declarations for special occasions—birth of His nation, dictating the ten commandments, His son's baptism, stuff like that.

He prefers to speak to people in less spectacular ways, using prophets, teachers, friends, family, circumstances, and times of inner silence and prayer to speak to our hearts.

Guess Who's Talking To help your child think about what it means to recognize God's voice, show her how well she knows other people's voices. Using a portable tape recorder, make two-second recordings of ten people you think your child might know. You can tape the voices of characters from TV shows and movies, the President in a news conference, a popular singer, sports announcers, an aunt's or a friend's voice over the phone. When you've gotten all ten recordings, you are ready to play the game with her.

Tell her the object is to see how many of the ten voice samples she can correctly identify (you'll be amazed). Talk about how remarkable it is that in two seconds she can identify the owner of the voice from among the hundreds of voices she knows. Ask how she thinks that's possible?

Now talk about God's voice. Ask, "Have you ever heard God's voice? How do you know? How does God speak to you? What kinds of things does He say?"

51 ◆ God Is Like Water

Start a Water Fight

O God, you are my God, earnestly I seek you; my soul thirsts for you, my body longs for you, in a dry and weary land where there is no water.
(Psalm 63:1)

In hot dry weather you need to drink two gallons of water per day just to keep going. It's no wonder. Your body uses water for everything—temperature control, digestion, air filtering, waste disposal, cell manufacture, and if you're under age two, drooling. In fact, your body is about 70 percent water.

God is like water. He cools and refreshes, quenches our desires, flushes out all the junk in our lives. That is, He does all this if we take and drink Him.

Wet Fun   Water fights are easy to start on a hot day. For example, you and your child could wash the car together. While your child is hosing off the car, "accidentally" walk into the spray. With mock seriousness, accuse him of trying to get you wet, then start to walk toward him with that give-me-the-hose look. If he's like most kids, he'll give it to you—in the face. Run for a bucket you've stashed behind the car, then charge him with it. If he drops the hose, pick it up and start spraying him. The rest of the battle is up to the two of you.

When you're through soaking each other, dry off and recount the game play-by-play. Talk about why water is so much fun. Talk about why it's so important to us physically. Then talk about the idea that God is like water. Ask, "In what way is God like water? What happens when you 'pour' God into your life? What does that mean? How do you keep from becoming dehydrated?"

Self-Portraits

> As the deer pants for streams of water,
>   so my soul pants for you, O God. My soul
> thirsts for God, for the living God.
>   When can I go and meet with God?
> (Psalm 42:1, 2)
> Everyone who drinks this water will be thirsty
> again, but whoever drinks the water I give
> him will never thirst. Indeed, the water I give
> him will become in him a spring of water
> welling up to eternal life.
> (Jesus, John 4:13, 14)